CHANNEL FISH

Cover illustration from a painting by Jean de Garis

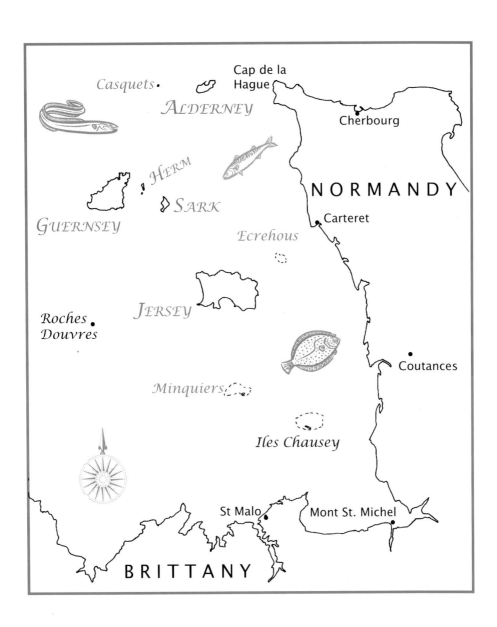

Casquets•
Cap de la
Hague
ALDERNEY
Cherbourg

HERM

SARK

NORMANDY

Carteret

GUERNSEY

Ecrehous

JERSEY

Roches•
Douvres

Coutances

Minquiers

Iles Chausey

St Malo•
Mont St. Michel

BRITTANY

CHANNEL FISH

A book of Fish Cookery
from the Channel Islands

Marguerite Paul

Illustrations by Charlotte Harris

Marguerite Paul

3. 11. 01

SEAFLOWER BOOKS

Published in 2001 by
SEAFLOWER BOOKS
1 The Shambles
Bradford on Avon
Wiltshire
BA15 1JS
www.ex-librisbooks.co.uk

Design and typesetting by
Seaflower Books

Printed in Britain by
Cromwell Press
Trowbridge
Wiltshire

ISBN 1 903341 10 8

Give a man a fish
And he'll eat for a day
Teach a man to fish
And he'll eat for a life-time

CONTENTS

CRUSTACEANS

MOLLUSCS

CEPHALOPODS

SOME HERBS, STOCKS, SAUCES, BUTTERS AND DIPS

Introduction

'In islands like Guernsey, the population is composed of men who have passed their lives in going around their fields, and of men who have passed their lives going around the world. There are two kinds of labourers, the tillers of the land and the toilers of the sea.'

Victor Hugo: *Toilers of the Sea*

What are my reasons for writing this book? The first falls into the 'red rag to a bull' category!

Our daughter, Odette, was at our favourite west coast beach when one of her friends – a keen amateur fisherman – offered her a handsome, very much alive, chancre crab, fresh from his pots. Her reply: "No thanks, I wouldn't know what to do with it!" shocked me. My daughter, a Guernsey girl, didn't know what to do with with such simple and delicious seafood.

I began to wonder how other young people might react, not only to the offer of a crab, but to any other of the wide variety of fish and shellfish found in local waters. Was there a need to better inform our young people about this wonderful resource?

The second reason followed on naturally from the first – in this health-conscious age, while there is general awareness of the great nutritional value of fish, there seems to be growing apprehension about buying and preparing it – thanks, in part at least, to the advent of convenience food! This book is therefore about encouraging people to be brave enough to visit a fishmonger and to enjoy this rich, *natural,* harvest on our doorstep.

Third, I am writing because of my love for my native Channel Islands and their heritage; the 'toilers of the sea' about whom Victor Hugo wrote while in Guernsey, certainly appreciated the bounty of local waters – why not us? Fishing methods and lifestyles may have changed but the fish that swim in our seas are every bit as good as they were in the 'good old days' and remain a wonderful source of raw material for an endless variety of delicious and healthy meals.

Before starting on the recipes, some basic facts on the geography and history of the Channel Islands – 'these little pieces of France dropped into the sea and collected by England', as Hugo put it.

Geography

The archipelago, known as the Channel Islands, was formed some 9,000 years ago as the sea rose following the end of the Ice Age – an earlier Global warming no doubt!

Powerful, surging tides – up to 7.8 knots (9mph) in the Race of Alderney, for example – and a rise and fall of 40 feet, during spring tides around Jersey, are the dominant characteristics of the sea in the area. The prevailing wind is from the south-west. Sea conditions frequently are not for the fainthearted and the inexperienced sailor would do well to avoid the Channel Islands. The courage, endurance and skill of our ancestors, when traversing and fishing these waters, with only sail and oars for propulsion and with minimal navigational aids, demands our admiration. Not surprisingly, the Channel Islands are the graveyard of many ships from the earliest of times and, indeed, the remains of a Gallo-Roman vessel – dubbed the *Asterix* – which foundered off St Peter Port in about 250 AD, were discovered and finally recovered from the entrance to the present harbour in the early 1980s. Stories of other wrecks and drownings abound.

A glance at the map (see frontispiece) shows the position of the islands within the Bay of St Malo and it is this positioning that creates, amongst other things, local variations of both marine habitat and therefore species of fish.

The waters between Jersey and the nearby coast of France are significantly shallower than those around Guernsey, Sark and Alderney – just to the north of which lies the Hurd Deep. At the same time, nutrients in the alluvial deposits emanating from the rivers and streams of neighbouring France – for example, the rivers Rance and Treguier – have a greater concentration in the waters surrounding Jersey than those around further-off Guernsey and Alderney, notwithstanding the fact that Alderney is the closest of all the Channel Islands to mainland France. The relatively little known Minquiers Plateau (called locally the Minkies), a shoal area half-way between Jersey and St Malo, is arguably the most southerly of the Channel Islands and, quaintly, boasts the southernmost toilet in the British Isles!

While the Channel Islands, generally, benefit from the warming effects of the Gulf Stream, local variations in water temperature (Jersey waters are slightly warmer, Alderney's colder) differing 'bottom' conditions and tidal ranges (Alderney's is only about half that of Jersey) also play their role in encouraging particular species. For example, whelks are found in abundance close to Jersey but are relatively unknown in Guernsey waters.

History

At the time of the Norman conquest of England in 1066, the islands formed part of the Duchy of Normandy and have remained loyal to the British Crown ever since. However, strong linguistic, family, commercial and cultural ties with France flourished until the 20th Century, with French being the official language in Guernsey until 1924. Norman patois was widely spoken within the islands until relatively recently but it is now, sadly, disappearing (hopefully, local enthusiasts in both Jersey and Guernsey will ensure some patois survival). In recent years, local people have come to regard England as the 'mainland' and most TV aerials in the Channel Islands point that way!

Fishing around the islands must have happened from the earliest times and the catching, drying, salting and exporting of fish (mainly conger eel and mackerel) was a major commercial activity in the medieval period – and Guernsey place names – Pecqueries Bay and Pezeries at Pleinmont, for example – remind us of fish drying activities of old, while salting took place at the 'Salerie Corner'.

Over time, in addition to fishing, a wide variety of other commercial actities has flourished in the Channel Islands including privateering (a kind of licensed piracy), smuggling, shipbuilding, quarrying, grape, tomato, potato and flower growing, cattle breeding, knitting (the ubiquitous 'jersey' needs no introduction when it comes to pullovers) and of course, tourism.

Today, however, the islands' economies rely hugely on the provision of 'offshore' financial services.

The export of grapes and stone and much else has long since gone – horticulture (remember the 'Guernsey Tom'?) and tourism (but no longer the bucket and spade variety) have dwindled but still play a role and there is also some light industry. Fortunately, the Jersey Royal (potato) remains a household name.

While fishing no longer enjoys it former importance, the latest official statistics show that, paradoxically, over the last six years, the reported catches of Guernsey registered fishing vessels actually increased in value from £2.9m to £3.3m in 1999, notwithstanding increasing competition, fish conservation measures, age old fisheries disputes, changing lifestyles and attractive alternative employment opportunities for local people. The bulk of the catch is delivered direct to mainland France. With the increasing efficiency of modern equipment, the local fishing industry employs far fewer people than in the past.

Sadly, St Peter Port's wonderful market, where fishmongers once jostled for space, has finally reached its 'best before' date and is about to be redeveloped – victim of planning decisions, changing shopping patterns and the motor car! The outcome of the market's forthcoming redevelopment is awaited with some apprehension. In Jersey, the situation is better and thriving 'traditional' retail fishmongers continue to ply their trade in St Helier's splendid Town Markets.

Thankfully, it is still possible to buy good fresh locally caught fish in Guernsey, as well as in the other islands, and if enough of us do just that then this part of our heritage will surely survive.

This book is dedicated to that aim

~   ~   ~

Some Fishy Advice

I shall divide what is fished from the sea into the following sections: Fish, Crustaceans, Molluscs and Cephalopods. I shall also include some recipes for smoked and preserved fish and other delicacies made from fish and shellfish not found in our waters.

A Guide to how much per person

Often it is confusing to know how much fish should be bought per person. What is a portion? The fishmonger can be very helpful but it is good to have an idea about how much you need to buy. Some fish is richer than others. For example, a smaller portion of salmon would be needed compared to whiting. Also, it depends if a fish will be served as a starter or a main course. Quantities are for one person.

	Starter	Main Course
Whole small fish	1	2 small or 1 larger
Large fish	120-180g	180-270g
(to be cooked whole)	4-6oz	6-9oz
e.g. bass		
Fillets or portions	90-120g	150-250g
e.g. plaice or cod	3-4oz	5-8oz
Crab (with shell)	250-375g	375-500g
	8-12oz	12-16oz
Crab (without shell)	60-90g	120-180g
	2-3oz	4-6oz
Smaller shellfish	200-250g	250-370g
e.g. mussels	7-8oz	8-12oz

Ways of Cooking

There are many ways of cooking fish but the simplest and quickest is often best. Having said that, care in preparation and presentation is essential.

Pan frying is quick and it seals the juices. I use a mixture of equal quantities of butter and olive oil. Once cooked, all the dish needs is a wedge of lemon or a simple home-made sauce which doesn't necessarily mean a hollandaise or béarnaise. These are wonderful sauces but slightly more complicated and, maybe, they should be reserved for the special occasion. Other methods are deep-frying, grilling (includes barbecuing), braising, poaching, simmering, baking/roasting, steaming, stir-frying and microwaving.

Some fish (e.g. tuna) and shellfish (e.g. oysters) may be enjoyed raw. Other fish may have been processed in some way, (e.g. by smoking) but may also require further cooking (e.g. kipper).

Conversion Tables

Some people still prefer to use imperial rather than metric units. I shall use both.

Oven temperatures are in centigrade and Fahrenheit and gas marks.

I haven't included Agas as some are two door while others are four. Most owners know and understand their Agas knowing which is the right oven to use when the reference is made to hot or medium.

The gram/ounce conversions are not exact but very close. This can be very confusing as 500g isn't exactly 1lb, so don't think that 2lbs is a kilo. For ease I am using 30g for 1oz. It is very close and easy to multiply e.g. 3 oz = 90g

Weight

For Ease	British Weight
30 grammes	1 oz
120 grammes	4 oz
250 grammes	8 oz
375 grammes	12 oz
500 grammes	1 lb
750 grammes	1 lb 8 oz
900 grammes	2 lbs
1 kilo	2.2 lbs

Liquid

British Imperial				For Ease
160 fl oz	8 pints	1 gallon	4.546 litres	4.4 litres
40 fl oz	2 pints	1 quart	1.136 litres	1 litre
20 fl oz	1 pint	4 gills	568 ml	550 ml
10 fl oz	$\frac{1}{2}$ pint	2 gills	284 ml	275 ml
5 fl oz	$\frac{1}{4}$ pint	1 gill	142 ml	150 ml
2 fl oz			56 ml	55 ml

Here are a few useful liquid measurements. I have rounded them up or down for ease:

1 litre = 10 decilitres(dl) = 100 centilitres (cl) = 1000 millilitres (ml)
1 litre = 40 fl oz
$\frac{1}{2}$ litre = 20 fl oz
$\frac{1}{4}$ litre = 10 fl oz
5 fl oz or 150 ml = 10 tablespoonfuls
$\frac{1}{2}$ fl oz or   15 ml =   1 tablespoonful
10 ml = 1 dessertsp
 5 ml = 1 teaspoon

Temperature Equivalents

Centigrade	Fahrenheit	Gas	
110 degrees	225 degrees	$\frac{1}{2}$	Cool
130 degrees	250 degrees	1	Very slow
140 degrees	275 degrees	1	Very slow
150 degrees	300 degrees	2	Slow
170 degrees	325 degrees	3	Moderate
180 degrees	350 degrees	4	Moderate
190 degrees	375 degrees	5	Moderately hot
200 degrees	400 degrees	6	Fairly hot
220 degrees	425 degrees	7	Hot
230 degrees	450 degrees	8	Very hot
240 degrees	475 degrees	9	Very hot
250 degrees	500 degrees	9	Extremely hot
270 degrees	525 degrees	9	Extremely hot

Measurements

1 inch	=	2.5 cm
2 inch	=	5 cm
6 inch	=	15 cm
12 inch	=	30 cm
39 inch	=	1 metre

Preparation

Suppose that a kind friend has been fishing and gives you some mackerel, a whiting or bass, or maybe you have been tempted by seeing whole fish on the fishmonger's slab. (Buying a whole fish on the bone is less expensive.) Having purchased or been given your fish comes the next dilemma, "What do I do, how do I start?" It is whole and complete and will probably need scaling and, worse still, gutting! At least a fish is neat with all the gut in the belly. Before starting, make sure you have a sharp knife, especially if you are going to fillet it, and a newspaper, as this absorbs any liquid. Once the gutting and scaling is finished all the waste can be wrapped up and disposed of.

Scaling

This can be done by using a fish scaler or a large knife or even an ormer or scallop shell. Recently I discovered to my cost that it is wise, first of all, to cut away any nasty, spiny looking dorsal or pelvic fins. Those are the fins along the back or under the body. The fish I was scaling was a black bream which has particularly nasty spiny fins. As I scraped away at the scales I caught my finger on one of the spiny fins – it was jolly painful too! Cut off the fins with a pair of scissors, then firmly grasp the tail and, using short sharp movements, get your knife under the scales pushing against them. You will find they come away easily. To make sure all have been removed run your fingers along the body. Rinse the fish under running water, then lay it on a board or slab in readiness for gutting. Even if you plan to cut off the head, it is easier to scale while whole.

Gutting

I find it is easier to have the belly facing the top of the board as you can see into the fish more easily. Scrape out the innards. If it looks as if there is a lot of blood around the back-bone, cut the covering membrane and scrape it out. Now rinse the whole of the cavity under running water making sure as much blood as possible is removed as this can taint the flesh.

If you plan to cook the fish without the head, cut off the head just behind the gills before gutting it. Now slit the belly and scrape away the innards in the same way as above.

The head can be left on if you plan to fillet the fish.

Skinning and Filleting

Round Fish

If the fish is to be cooked whole or headless, the skin is left on as it keeps the flesh moist. Once cooked, if you want to remove it, it is easily peeled off, revealing steaming succulent flesh.

There are two ways of filleting a small fish and in a way it is a question of which way you feel happier, holding the head or the tail. I like to hold the tail, easing the knife up to the gills. Others prefer to hold the head, inserting the knife just behind the head and keeping the knife as flat as possible and using short strokes, easing it down to the tail. Whichever way you choose, once you get going lay your hand flat on the fillet to prevent it from moving, but take care.

If you have a big fish, which is too big to hold by its head or tail, it is easier to start by using the knife to make a cut under the dorsal fin and, with gentle movements, ease the knife along the upper part of the fish, easing it down the backbone and down to the belly. Now the fillet can be skinned or left as it is and cut into portions.

To skin a fillet such as haddock, lay the fillet on a board, skin side down, and make a small cut at the tail down to the skin, keeping the blade angled almost flat agains the skin, gradually ease the knife up towards the thicker flesh. The beginning is the most difficult but once you get going it is easy.

Flat Fish

This method of skinning is for a plaice or sole when the fish is going to be cooked whole with the meat on the bone.

Lay the fish dark side up. At the tail end, make two cuts crossing each other so that the point is towards you. Ease your finger in lifting the skin from the flesh, ease your finger along both sides to loosen it, now take a firm hold of the skin in one of your hands. Using the other, hold the tail and with sharp movements pull the dark skin towards the head. It might be easier to wrap a piece of kitchen towel around the slippery tail to get a firmer grip.

The more delicate white underside skin is usually left on the fish.

There are two ways to fillet a flat fish. If it is small, start from the tail. Make an incision, ease the knife under and keeping it as flat as possible work up towards the head.

If it is a large fish, cut along the backbone easing the fillet away by long sideways strokes from head to tail till you reach the fins at the top. Turn the fish around and remove the second fillet. Now turn it over and repeat the process.

Boning a small fish

Sometimes a fish is too small to be filleted and yet the thought of all those bones is off-putting. The method known as 'butterfly boning' is a good way to get the spine out, along with lots of the little bones attached to it.

Having gutted the fish, remove the head. Now, slit the belly opening down to the tail, lay it flat, belly side down, and with your palm flatten the fish, then gently with the heel of your hand press the whole length of the back bone. You will feel the back bone or spine relax, releasing the flesh. Turn the fish over and ease the back-bone off towards the tail taking all the smaller side bones with it. Any renegade bones left behind can be removed by hand with tweezers or small pliers.

Shellfish

What is the kindest way to kill live shellfish?

I have discussed, with Herbert Nichols, a local fisherman, the kindest way of cooking crustaceans.

For small crustaceans such as shrimp and prawns, plunge them into a good quantity of boiling water. If you can get seawater that is the best but if not available, add to 1 litre of water 3 tbsps salt.

Bring back to the boil, gently boil for one minute, no longer. Strain and allow to cool.

Lobster and Crab (Chancres)

There are several ways of killing a crab or a lobster. My preferred way and which I recommend is to place the crab or lobster in luke warm water for 10 minutes. This makes it sleepy. After 10 minutes, lift it from the water and you will notice it is limp. This means it is dead. You will notice that the water may be a brownish colour. This is because the fish has purged itself which means it is clean within.

Now, place it in boiling salted water. Bring back to the boil and cook for 20 minutes.

Crayfish and Spider Crabs

These can be killed and cooked in the same way as crabs and lobsters.

Crayfish: Cook for 30 minutes once back to boiling point.

Spider crabs: Cook for 20 minutes once back to boiling point.

For the smaller shellfish such as mussels, scallops, ormers etc., I shall deal with as we reach them in each recipe.

Choosing Fish and Shellfish

We are fortunate in these islands to be able to buy very fresh, locally caught fish, sometimes, even, straight from the sea. Those of us who are anglers or have boats are perhaps the luckiest of all!

Always look for fish that has bright eyes and a shiny skin.

Ask you fishmonger's advice as to what is a good buy – after all, he is the expert and has his reputation to protect.

Ask for a fish that you know is in season – many species are available all year round but are only 'best' at certain times.

There is no overall rule of thumb – an 'r' in the month is not always a reliable indicator!

Having taken the trouble to buy fresh fish, it is best to enjoy it promptly although it can, of course, be stored temporarily, if kept chilled (see page 17).

You can even freeze your fish, but this rather defeats the object!

Frozen fish can be 'fresher' than fish bought at the fishmonger because, with modern equipment, fish is caught, gutted, processed (eg: prawns may have their shells removed), packed and frozen, all while at sea.

As always, when considering food, quality of the product is paramount but it is fine to use reputable brands of frozen or chilled fish with any of the recipes in this book.

Fish should not be left in the freezer for too long – respect the instructions on the package. If in doubt, use oily fish, such as salmon, within three months and other fish within six months.

Care must be taken with shellfish.

Crabs, lobsters and crayfish should always be alive, if possible.

Always eat cooked shellfish on the day of purchase. This also applies to picked shellfish.

A crab, lobster or crayfish should feel heavy. If it feels light it could be that it has been stored in a vivier or that it has shed its shell recently. After shedding its shell the flesh is watery and takes up to four months to become firm again.

A good guide is a shell that has tiny limpets or barnacles attached to it. Once again, be guided by your fishmonger.

Fresh prawns should be bright and a grey / green colour. They should be firm and the tail have spring in it, not limp or dull.

Bivalves, that is shellfish with two shells hinged at the base, need great care when buying. Whichever you buy, make sure the shell is very tightly closed. This applies to scallops and mussels but fortunately with mussels, any that don't open on cooking means they are no good so should be thrown out.

Oysters are usually eaten raw so extra care must be taken over freshness – one has to be guided by the fishmonger. He may open or shuck them for you, make sure you eat them the same day.

Remember that the flesh of shellfish decomposes very quickly.

My recipes

They are not what a chef might create. They are straightforward, using simple ingredients and if a certain herb, for example, isn't available, then I use something else. When it comes to herbs, I tend to be extravagant as I love their different smells and the colour adds something special. A white sauce on a white fish looks dull but a handful of chopped parsley transforms it.

Most people enjoy eating fish but many prefer someone else to cook it! I hope that some of my recipes will encourage you to try.

If we have friends in, I invariably serve fish and it doesn't become a great hassle. I do have my favourite recipes which are ideal for supper parties. I want to enjoy the evening, not spend it sweating over the stove!

Just a word on sauces. Always try and make them runny rather than stodgy. A runny sauce is always a delight to mop up anyway.

~   ~   ~

FISH

Sea Bass

Sea Bass	*Dicentrarchus labrax*
Guernsey French	*barr* or *lubin* (m)
Jersey French	*bar* (m)
French	*loup de mer* or *bar commun* (m)

There is a Guernsey saying (at the end of the ploughing season):

'A quànd lé boeu est lâs, lé barr est gras.'
When the ox is weary, the bass is fat.

Bass was once considered a cheap alternative to cod. Now it commands quite a high price.

Bass is fished at sea from boats but line fishing from the shore has become more and more popular.

I live near Le Gouffre in Guernsey and enjoy walks on the cliff paths. Looking down I often see the rocks at La Moye Point dotted with fishermen even on the bleakest of days. The fishermen tend to favour sandy gullies as well as the rocky shore. I wonder how on earth they get down there and back! I believe that some of them stay overnight. The long, patient wait for the line to be dragged down can be rewarding in more ways than one as some of the competitions are very lucrative indeed. Added to the incentive of prize money, the bass is a fighter, so there is the excitement of playing it to the shore.

The deep swift-running waters around Alderney seem to favour bass as it is caught in large quantities.

It is an attractive medium-sized fish 36-75 cm / 14-30in. The smaller ones can be cooked whole, filleted or, if a larger specimen, cut into cutlets.

This streamlined fish is covered with steely grey scales on the back paling to silvery ones on the side to white on the underside.

It is available all year round but is best from June to February. Anglers fish for it from April to January. It has a good bone structure which makes it easy to handle. Having said that the texture of the flesh is not all that firm so it has to be dealt with carefully. The flavour is excellent.

Before cooking, the fish is normally scaled. Do this by firmly holding the fish by the tail and with a fish scaler or blunt edge of a knife, work towards the head with short sharp movements. Wash it under running cold water. If you can, do this outside as the scales fly everywhere and you'll be finding them for days after! The fish should now be gutted and filleted, cut right across for cutlets or left whole.

Barbecued Bass

This recipe is from Nick Jouault, a former fisherman and now marine conservationist in Jersey.

Take a large bass about $1\frac{1}{4}$ kilo /3 lbs.

Slit 4 or 5 times into the flesh and insert slices of garlic. Place on foil. Cover with crushed fennel seed, basil, oregano, dried piri piri (a very hot South American chilli), loads of soya sauce and a little olive oil.

Sliced onion covering the fish is an extra optional.

Carefully wrap it in the foil and lay on the barbecue for approximately 4 minutes on each side.

Tease the foil open to see that it is cooked but don't overcook.

Sea Bass fillets with Mushroom and Caper Sauce

To serve 4
Fillets of 180g / 6oz per person
1 tbsp chopped capers
120 grams / 4oz sliced mushrooms
Juice of 1 lemon
2 tbsp chopped parsley

2 tbsp cream
60g/2oz butter
30g/1oz flour
white wine or water
2 spring onions
1 clove garlic

Grease or oil the bottom of a roasting tin or ovenproof dish, lay the fillets skin side down. Season with salt/pepper. Sprinkle with chopped capers, lemon juice and a small knob of butter on each fillet. Add 150ml /$\frac{1}{4}$pt water or white wine. Cover with foil.

Bake in a preheated oven 200°C/ 400°F Gas 6 for 8-10 minutes.

While cooking make the mushroom sauce.

Finely chop a fat clove of garlic and finely slice the spring onions. Gently fry in a saucepan in 60 grams/2oz butter taking care not to burn it. Add the finely sliced mushrooms and cook until the juice runs.

Sprinkle over the 30grams/1oz flour mixing gently. When the fish is cooked, remove it from the oven and gently pour the juice from the pan into the roux.

Keep the fish warm while you finish the sauce. Stir gently until smooth. Add a little more wine if too thick. Finally add 2 tbsp cream and chopped parsley, bring almost to the boil and put to one side while serving the fish.

Place a fillet on each plate, cover generously with sauce.

Serve with new potatoes and a fresh tomato and basil salad.

Sea Bass Baked Whole with Cider Sauce

To serve 4

1 sea bass weighing $1\frac{1}{2}$ kg/3lbs

3tbsp chopped mixed herbs such as thyme, rosemary and sage

60g/2oz butter plus a bit extra for placing on the fish

275ml/10fl oz dry cider

1tbsp lemon juice

2tbsp cream

1small onion or 2 shallots

1 tbsp chopped parsley

30g/1 oz flour

Salt and pepper

Scale and clean the bass and cut 3 diagonal slashes on either side.

Lay the bass on a large strong piece of foil. Season both sides with salt, pepper, lemon juice and 2 tbsp of chopped herbs, making sure as much as possible goes inside the slashes. Dot the fish with butter and wrap it up with the join on the top.

Carefully lift into a roasting tin, add a little water as this helps to prevent sticking.

Bake in a preheated hot oven at 215C/425F Gas 7 for 30 minutes.

Meanwhile make the sauce.

Fry a small onion or two shallots in the butter. Add the flour, mix well then add the cider, lemon juice and the final tbsp of mixed herbs. Season. When smooth and bubbling set aside.

When the fish is cooked, carefully lift it from the tin and lay on the serving dish. Roll back the foil, crinkling it around the fish. Quickly reheat the sauce, add the cream and tbsp chopped parsley.

Serve the sauce separately.

A courgette and red pepper salad would go well.

Fry one red and one green pepper that have been thinly sliced and deseeded in olive oil. Add a sliced courgette or two and cook till all have collapsed. Sprinkle 1 tsp ground cumin, a handful of chopped flat leaf parsley and two finely sliced spring onions. Season.

Cool and serve.

Sea Bass with Pernod Sauce

To serve 4

4 fillets of Sea Bass each weighing approx 250g/8oz
1 fennel bulb
2 finely sliced spring onions
2 tbsp olive oil
2 skinned and finely chopped tomatoes
2/3tbsp Pernod or other aniseed flavoured liquor such as Ricard or
   Arrak
Chives
Extra butter and oil for cooking.

Split the fennel bulb down the middle, finely slice it and in a saucepan or frying pan gently soften it in 2 tbsps olive oil. Add 2 finely sliced spring onions and 2 finely chopped tomatoes. Season. Add 275ml/ 10fl oz water and allow to simmer until pulpy and soft. Add more water if it begins to stick. Cook for about 30 minutes or until thick.

When thick, add the Pernod or similar.

Meanwhile, oil or butter a grill pan or baking dish. Lay the Sea Bass fillets skin side down, season and drizzle with olive oil or dot with butter. Grill for 10 minutes or bake for 10 minutes in a hot oven.

Place the aniseed flavoured tomato mixture in a serving dish, lay the fillets carefully on top. Scissor a few chives on each fillet and serve.

Alternatively, place a fillet on each plate with the tomato mixture alongside.

New potatoes or sautéed potatoes would go very well with this dish.

A good salad is a couple of fennel bulbs that have been very finely sliced or briefly whizzed in the food processor (it is exhausting if you have to crunch your way through large pieces). Add 60g/2 oz finely chopped gruyère cheese, 2 or 3 finely sliced spring onions, salt and pepper and 2 tbsp chopped parsley.

Dress with a vinaigrette that has been made with lemon juice rather than vinegar.

Sea Bream

Black Sea Bream	*Spondyliosoma cantharus*
Guernsey french	*sarde naër* (f), *brême* (f)
Jersey French	*brême* (f), *sarde* (f)
French	*dorade* (f)

There are several species of sea bream found in our waters. The black is the most common. Couch's Sea Bream – *Pagrus pagrus* and Red Sea Bream – *Pagellus bogaraves* are also seen in these waters.

A deep bodied scaly fish, up to 50 cm long. The black bream, which seems to be increasing in numbers, is really dark grey with a grey/black back, silvery sides and dusky vertical bars along back and sides. It likes a rocky coast where it can grind shells with its sharp protruding teeth. It is a delicious fish and popular with anglers. Often fishing takes place at night, up to a mile or so from the shore. In times gone by, fishermen would go at night to the 'bottom of the bay' that is about half to 1 mile out. Using garden snails (*des colimâchaöns*) for bait, they would fish with lines from their boats. Now the frill from around a scallop is often used for bait.

Before choosing a recipe, the fish needs to be scaled and the spiny dorsal and ventral fins removed. The dorsal fin is particularly spiny. The last bream I scaled got me, and it was one of those spiny fins! Jolly painful too!

Start by removing the fins with a pair of scissors. Now scale and gut the fish. It is easy to gut as everything comes out neat and compact.

Sea bream can be cooked whole or filleted – grill, bake, fry or barbecue.

It is available all year round but is at its best from October until early Spring.

You will need 1 plump bream for 2 people. If they are on the small side, then one per person.

A fisherman friend told me that a gutted but not scaled Sea Bream wrapped in damp newspaper and baked in the oven for half an hour is delicious. As you peel back the newspaper, the scales come away too.

Grilled or Fried Fillets of Black Sea Bream with Courgettes

Serves 4

2 bream weighing approx 500g/1 lb each or 1 bream weighing approx $1\frac{1}{2}$ kilo/3 lbs

Alternatively 4 plump fillets – if on the small side, use 8

750g/$1\frac{1}{2}$ lbs courgettes

250g/8 oz mushrooms	Seasoned flour for tossing the fillets in
1 medium onion	3 tbsp olive oil and knob of butter for frying
1 tbsp fresh coriander	Wedges of lemon
1 tbsp fresh parsley	Salt and pepper

Remove the spiny fins with a pair of scissors before filleting.

Fillet the bream by laying them on their side and easing the knife down from the (removed) dorsal fin to release the fillet. Turn the fish around and repeat so that you have a good sized fillet. Cut it down the middle. I find it easier filleting a bream this way rather than starting from the tail. You should aim to get four good-sized fillets.

Finely slice the onion and gently fry in 1tbsp olive oil, until softened. Keep warm.

Slice the courgettes into the pan and gently fry, adding a little extra oil if necessary. Remove.

Next fry the sliced mushrooms till the juice runs. Add the onions, chopped coriander and parsley. Season, gently turning to mix. Remove from the pan and add to the fried courgettes. Keep warm.

In the same pan add 2 tbsps oil and a knob of butter. Fry the dried and flour coated fillets, pushing them gently until sealed and browned.

Turn when cooked, approx 3 to 4 minutes each side.

Serve on the bed of courgettes and mushroom mixture with wedges of lemon.

Alternatively, place a fillet on each plate with the courgette and mushroom mixture alongside.

Serve with rice or potatoes cooked the way you like best.

Baked Sea Bream with Tomatoes and Potatoes

To serve 4	Juice of 1 lemon
1 Bream 1$\frac{1}{2}$ kilo / 3lbs	3/4 spring onions
1 kilo/2lbs potatoes	Ground cumin
500g/1lb tomatoes	1 tbsp olive oil
Fresh thyme and parsley	Salt and pepper

Peel and fairly finely slice the potatoes, place in boiling water for 5 minutes until cooked. May take less time depending on the type but don't overcook. Drain.

Skin and chop the tomatoes, fry in a little olive oil until becoming mushy.

Oil an oven-proof dish and cover bottom with the potato and tomato mixture, sprinkle with chopped fresh thyme and sliced spring onions, season.

Take the scaled and cleaned bream. Cut three diagonal slices down to the bone. Season. Lay it on the mixture in the oven-proof dish. Dust with ground cumin, season, sprinkle with lemon juice and olive oil and place in a hot oven 220C/425F Gas 7 for 30 minutes until sizzling and golden.

Sprinkle with parsley and serve.

A tossed green salad goes well.

If you prefer, you can use skinned fillets. Lay them on top of the tomato and potato mixture and finish in the same way.

Baked or Grilled Sea Bream with Spiced Rice

To serve 4

1bream weighing1½ kilo /3lbs
1heaped tsp ground coriander
1heaped tsp ground cumin
Salt and pepper
250g/8ozs basmati rice
6 cloves

6 whole cardamom pods
Piece cinnamon stick
2/3 bay leaves
1 small onion
1 clove garlic
2 tbsp olive oil
Wedges of lemon

Prepare the rice first.

If you happen to have a heavy-duty pan or ovenproof casserole do use it as this saves the washing-up!

In the casserole, fry the chopped onion and garlic in 1tbsp olive oil until transparent. Add the rice and gently fry for 2 minutes. Add the cloves, cardamom, cinnamon, bay leaves, 1 tsp salt and plenty ground black pepper.

Cover the rice with water. Put on the lid or cover with foil and cook for 30-40 minutes in a medium oven 180C/350F Gas 4 for 30 minutes.

Check. If the rice is still wet put back in the oven for 5-10 minutes. The rice should be dry. If, on the other hand, you find that it is a bit stuck to the bottom, add 2 tbsp water. Don't stir the rice, just leave it to rest and it will soon relax and release its grip on the pan.

While the rice is cooking, rinse the bream and pat dry. Make 3 diagonal slashes on both sides. Oil a baking dish or grill pan. Lay the fish in. Sprinkle both sides with ground cumin and coriander. Season, drizzle with 1 tbsp olive oil and bake in a hot oven 220C/425F Gas 7 for 30 minutes or grill under a hot grill turning half way through.

Place on a serving dish, surrounded with wedges of lemon.

Serve with the spiced rice and ratatouille or a mixture of fried tomatoes and onions with a final scattering of thyme.

BRILL

Brill	*Scophthalmus rhombus*
Guernsey French	*brille* (f)
Jersey French	*brille* (f), *cat* (m)
French	*barbue* (f)

Brill seems to have the reputation of being the country cousin to turbot. In fact it is a delicious fish and a real treat. It tends to be expensive but is definitely worth the extra cost.

Brill is a flat fish, found in shallow sandy water. It is sandy coloured with darker spots so that from above, it looks like the seabed it lives on. There can be confusion over the difference between turbot and brill. Brill has a smooth upper skin whereas turbot has little nodules. If you run your finger down the back of a turbot, you will feel them as opposed to the smoothness of the brill. Its underbody is white and it grows up to 50/60cms long. Its flesh is creamy coloured.

It is available all year round but is best during the summer months.

Brill is best served as fillets as they are easier to handle. Serving a whole fish creates problems because it is difficult to reach the underside.

 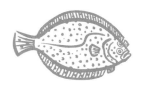 

Baked Brill with Shrimp Sauce

Serves 4
4 brill fillets each weighing approx 180g/ 6 oz
150ml/ 5 fl oz white wine
60g/ 2 oz butter

Sauce:

60g/2oz butter	2tbsp chopped dill
30g/1oz plain flour	Juice of half a lemon
150ml/5fluid oz milk	2 tbsp cream
120g/4oz cooked chopped shrimps or a 200g tin	Salt and pepper

Butter an ovenproof dish. Lay the fillets in a row.

Using the remaining butter, dot each fillet. Season. Add the wine and same quantity of water. Cover with foil. Place in a moderate oven 190C, 375F Gas 5 for 20 minutes.

To make the sauce: Melt 60g/ 2oz butter, remove from heat and add the flour to make a roux. Gradually stir in the liquor from the dish, holding back the brill. Cover it while the sauce is finished. Add the milk to the sauce bringing it slowly to the boil, stirring till smooth and thickened.

Add the chopped shrimps or tin of shrimp, the dill and lemon juice. Mix till well distributed.

Add the cream and if the sauce is still too thick, add a little white wine, the aim is to have a fairly runny sauce. Check seasoning. Cover to keep hot.

Serve each fillet with the sauce poured over and around. Any remaining sauce, serve separately.

 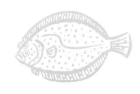 

Brill with White Wine and Lemon Thyme

Serves 4

4 fillets each weighing approx.180g/ 6oz
White breadcrumbs – a good 30g/1oz

60g/2oz butter	1 tbsp chopped lemon thyme
Extra melted butter for brushing fillets	1 tbsp flour
4 spring onions	Juice of 2 lemons
4 tbsp chopped parsley	2 tbsp cream
275ml /10fluid oz dry white wine	Salt and pepper

Butter a grill-pan or oven-proof dish.

Having washed and dried the brill fillets, brush with melted butter, coat with bread-crumbs and lay in the grill pan or oven-proof dish.

Using half the butter, divide into four and dot each fillet. Add the lemon juice, season and pour around half of the white wine.

Place in a preheated oven 230C/450F Gas 8 for 20 minutes. After 10 minutes turn the fish, scattering them with the chopped spring onions and cook for the final 10 minutes.

If grilling, cook for 5 minutes, turn and scatter with chopped spring onions. Grill for a further 5 minutes.

I like the spring onions to have a slightly charred look and flavour.

Cover with foil to keep warm.

In a saucepan, melt the other half of butter. Add the flour and mix until smooth. Add the juice from the pan or grill and the remaining half of wine. When bubbling and smooth, remove from the heat add the chopped parsley and lemon thyme, check seasoning, add the cream. This is a very lemony sauce.

Place a fillet on each plate and surround with sauce.

Serve with new potatoes and spinach to which you have added 2 tbsps cream and a dusting of nutmeg.

Brill with a Red Wine Sauce

And now a red wine sauce. Brill happily marries with both red and white wine.

Serves 4

4 fillets of brill, each weighing approx 180g/ 6 oz

1 medium onion or 3 or 4 shallots	5 or 6 juniper berries (optional)
275ml/ 10 fl oz red wine	3 leeks
2 tbsp red wine vinegar	60g/2 oz butter
120g/4 oz butter	Salt and pepper

Butter an ovenproof dish, just big enough so that the fillets fit snugly. Barely cover with water. Season with salt and pepper. Cover with foil and cook in a hot oven 230C, 450F,

Gas 8 for 15/20 minutes.

While the brill is cooking, finely chop the onion or shallot and put in a small saucepan with the red wine, vinegar and crushed juniper berries. Simmer for 10 minutes.

Once the fish is cooked, gently strain the cooking liquid in with the red wine mixture. Cover the fish to keep warm.

Trim the leeks and cut into thin julienne strips and sweat in 60g/ 2oz butter for five minutes. Keep warm.

Boil the liquor until very much reduced, and syrupy. Away from the heat, beat in the butter in small lumps.

Place a fillet of brill on each plate and a small pile of leeks.

Tastefully anoint each plate with the wine sauce.

Brill with a Tomato Salsa

Serves 4

8 fillets each weighing approx 90g/3oz or 4 larger pieces each weighing approx 180g/6oz. For this recipe, keep the skin on.

60g/2 oz butter

For the Salsa	Salt and pepper
4 large ripe tomatoes	A few drops tabasco
4 spring onions	Juice of half a lemon
1 avocado	2 tbsp olive oil
2 tbsp chopped parsley	Chives

Make the salsa first.

Skin the tomatoes by placing them in a bowl, pouring boiling water over. After 1 minute, slip the skins off. Cut in half and, with a teaspoon, remove and discard the seeds.

Chop the tomato finely and put into a serving bowl.

Cut the avocado in half, remove the stone and very finely cut crisscross. Gently scoop out the flesh into the bowl with the tomatoes. Now finely slice the spring onions, and along with the chopped parsley add to the tomato mixture.

The smoother you want the salsa, the finer the chopping. Season. Add a few drops of tabasco. Add the olive oil and lemon juice. Cover with cling film and chill until needed.

Butter a grill pan or ovenproof dish. Lay the brill fillets skin side up. Season and place knobs of butter on each. Place under a hot grill for 4/5 minutes or in an oven 200C/400F Gas 6 for 10 minutes. Half way through cooking, glaze with the buttery juice from the pan.

The aim is a dark crusty skin. Check to make sure it is cooked.

Plate with the skin upper most and the remainder of the buttery liquid poured over. Scissor a handful of chives on each fillet.

Serve with the salsa and plenty of fresh bread.

A green salad too, perhaps a mixture of salad leaves with some rocket for its pepperiness.

COD

Cod	*Gadus Morhua*
Guernsey French	*mouarue* (f)
Jersey French	*mouothue* (f)
French	*morue* (f), *cabillaud*

Cod is a handsome fish which can grow up to 1.5 m in length. It has a long barbel under the chin, three dorsal and two ventral fins. The back and sides are mottled greeny-grey with a white underneath. The flesh is very white and has excellent texture and flavour – the emergence in Britain of 'Fish and Chips', as part of the national diet, is testimony to the wide popularity of cod ! The medicinal benefits of cod liver oil have long been recognised.

Cod tend to be filleted or cut into steaks – either way, the few bones are easy to handle. The head and bones make excellent stock for soup and sauces. Cod roe can be used in many ways.

Cod is available all year round but is best in the winter months.

By the 16th Century, local fishing boats were making the long voyage to Newfoundland, cashing in on the abundant cod in those waters. During its heyday, cod fishing off Newfoundland created many a small fortune locally and probably helped develop the distinctive St Peter Port skyline that we know today.

Before refrigeration, the drying and salting of cod was big business. Even today, dried cod is still available and is particularly enjoyed by the Portuguese.

People believed that cod stocks were unlimited but, inevitably, this proved not to be the case and so, by 1822, as a result of a severe decline in catches, it was found necessary to establish an international Convention introducing 2 mile territorial 'fishing limits'. However, in 1958, Iceland increased her territorial water to 12 miles, thus starting the "Cod Wars" which saw confrontation between well equipped Icelandic patrol boats and ships of the British Navy.

Thankfully, cod stocks now seem to be improving.

Cod was never a particularly plentiful fish in Channel Island waters.

Battered Cod

Serves 4
4 portions filleted cod each approx. 180/250g - 6/8 oz

Batter: There are two types, one made with yeast and one without. Both need to be made well in advance of the actual cooking. They must be really thick so that they coat the fish.

Unleaven Batter
90g/3oz plain flour
120ml / 4fl oz of either a mixture of milk and water or beer and water
1 egg
1tbsp melted butter
Pinch salt
Whisk the egg then add the flour. Gradually add the liquid, holding back if necessary as you want a thick creamy mixture. Rest it for as long as possible.

Yeast Batter
As fresh yeast is difficult to find, I use loose dried yeast, though the small packets can be used too.

150 ml /5 fl oz beer
1 tsp dried or packeted yeast
120g/4oz plain flour
salt and pepper

Sprinkle the yeast on the warmed beer in a mixing bowl. Leave until it bubbles. Add the flour and mix until smooth. Leave to prove, approx 1 hour.   If using packeted yeast, mix all the ingredients until smooth and leave to prove approx 1 hour. Once again, aim for a really thick batter. Add more flour if necessary. On the other hand, if the batter is too thick, add a little more beer or water. Use in the same way as the unleaven batter.

The temperature of the cooking oil is most important. If the oil isn't hot enough it results in a greasy soggy mass. On the other hand if it is too hot, the batter will be dark brown and hard and the fish inside undercooked.

Heat the oil in a deep fryer or saucepan to 160C/325F. Drop a blob of batter in and, if it sizzles straight away, the oil is ready. Don't let the oil reach smoking point.

Coat the cod in batter and using a slotted spoon, gently immerse in the oil. Two pieces at a time is enough.

Cook for 6/7 minutes till crisp and golden brown.

Drain on absorbent paper. Keep hot but uncovered till all are cooked.

Serve with wedges of lemon and tartare sauce.

There is also HP Sauce and Tomato Ketchup, both of which have stood the test of time! Malt vinegar too.

Cod with Mushrooms

Serves 4

4 cod steaks each approx.180g/6oz	1 medium onion
60g/2oz brown breadcrumbs	90g/3oz butter
1 tbsp chopped parsley	Juice of half a lemon
375g/12oz mushrooms	Salt and pepper

Butter an ovenproof dish. Lay the cod steaks in the dish. Sprinkle with lemon juice. Spread the breadcrumbs on each steak pressing down so that a crust is formed. Place a knob of butter on each.

As a variation, use pieces or fillets rather than steaks with skin left on. Cook in the same way as the steaks.

Cook in a hot oven 200C/400F Gas 6 for 15-20 minutes or under a hot grill, until the crust is crisply roasted and golden.

Meanwhile, in the remaining butter, gently fry the chopped onion until transparent, add the sliced mushrooms, season. Finally, add the chopped parsley.

Keep warm.

To serve, place a cod steak on each plate with the mushroom and onion mixture and a dollop of tartare sauce or serve the tartare separately.

A bowl of buttered boiled potatoes goes well.

A colourful vegetable is some carrots that have been cut into matchstick pieces or finely sliced that have been slowly cooked in a little butter. On serving add a scattering of chopped parsley.

Normandy Cod with Tomato and Garlic Sauce

4 steaks or fillets each weighing approx 180g/6oz
1 tbsp Dijon mustard
300ml/10 fl oz white wine or dry cider

60g/ 2 oz butter
1 tbsp Calvados
1 tbsp lemon juice
Sauce
750g/ 1½ lbs tomatoes
3 cloves garlic

3 shallots or 1 small onion
1 tbsp chopped parsley
10 fresh basil leaves
1 tbsp lemon juice
30g/1oz butter
Salt and cayenne pepper

Butter an ovenproof dish. Spread the mustard on each steak or fillet. Lay in the dish. Season. Divide the butter into 4 and place a piece on each steak or fillet. Pour around the cider or white wine, lemon juice and calvados. Cover with foil.

Place in a hot oven 200C/400F Gas 6 and cook for 10 minutes covered, remove the foil for the final cooking, another 10 minutes.

To make the sauce. Fry the chopped shallots or onion and chopped garlic in the butter, taking care not to let the garlic burn. Add the remaining ingredients, including 6 torn or scissored basil leaves. Adjust the amount of cayenne to taste.

Allow to bubble gently until tomatoes are soft and pulpy. If you like a fine sauce pass through a sieve. Keep warm.

Remove the cod from the oven. Add the juice to the sauce.

Tear or scissor the remaining basil leaves on each piece of cod.

Serve with the sauce poured around or separately.

A bowl of buttered and parsleyed new potatoes and a tossed green salad goes well with the cod.

Pan Fried Cod

This is the simplest way of cooking cod and it can be served with many different sauces or just a wedge of lemon. I feel the plainer the better not to obscure the flavour or hide the flakes of succulent fish.

All you need is seasoned flour or seasoned breadcrumbs to coat the steaks or fillets. Fry them gently in a mixture of half oil and butter.

4 steaks or fillets need 2 tbsp oil and 60g/2oz butter

Heat the oil and butter mixture till hot. Add the cod and cook for about 5 minutes. Turn and cook the other side until golden brown.

Cod seems to go best with potatoes whether plain boiled, sautéed or browned in the oven.

The following recipe for potatoes is one I learnt from our cook in Morocco. Ever since then, they have been known by the family as 'Pommes à la Fidela'.

Take as many potatoes you think you will need. Peel and dice into sugar lump size. Place in a saucepan of cold water and bring to the boil. Parboil for 10/15 minutes. Drain.

Place in a roasting tin, sprinkle with salt and pepper, 2/3 tbsps olive oil, a good scattering of fresh or dried tarragon. At this point they can be left and finished off about an hour before you need them.

Cook in a hot oven 200C/400F Gas 6 until golden brown. Shake them every now and again.

Cod Nuggets for Kids

The quantity of fish depends on the age of the children but a guide would be about 90g/3oz per child.

Skin the fish and then cut into a suitable size for your children.

Toss the nuggets in flour (a plastic or paper bag with flour is neat and works).

Gently fry the nuggets in a mixture of butter and olive oil until golden brown and tender.

Drain on absorbent kitchen paper and serve with ketchup or whatever sauce the children like.

Cod with Chick Peas and Tomatoes

Cod nuggets cooked as in the above recipe but increase the quantity to 180g/6oz per person

Serves 4
2 spring onions
1 clove garlic
2 tbsp oil
500g/ 1 lb tomatoes or (1 tin chopped tomatoes)
Herbs such as thyme or oregano
Salt and pepper
400g tin of chick peas
Tabasco
1 tbsp chopped parsley

Slice the spring onions and chop the garlic and put in a frying pan. Add the oil and cook for a couple of minutes.

Add the chopped tomatoes and cook until soft and mushy, adding water if necessary.

Add herbs such as thyme, or oregano. Season, adding a few drops of tabasco.

Drain the chick peas and heat in a saucepan. Add a little water to prevent them sticking.

When hot, drain and scatter into a serving dish with the sauce poured over. Cover and keep warm.

Cook the cod nuggets. Place on top of the tomato and chick pea mixture.

Garnish with chopped parsley and serve.

COLEY

Coley, also known as
coalfish and saithe   *Pollachius virens*
G'sey french   *lu naër* (m) or *lu noir* (m)
Jersey french   *colin* (m)
French   *colin* (m), *lieu noir* (m)

A round fish similar to cod with a dark green back paling to a silver underside.

The flesh is greyish/white. It grows to 60-100cms/2-3ft. It is available all year round and is inexpensive.

Generally, it comes filleted. The flesh is firm like cod but greyer in colour. On cooking the colour pales significantly.

Like cod it can be fried or braised. Coley also makes a delicious fish pie either on its own or mixed with other fish. It can be as spicy or bland as you like. I tend to add a little smoked fish and shellfish such as prawns. This combination seems to appeal to children as well.

Hard boiled eggs can be chopped and added to the fish mixture.

Fish Pie

Cod or haddock may be used instead of coley

Serves 4
750g/1½ lbs coley
250g/8oz smoked haddock
120g/4oz cooked peeled prawns
2 hard boiled eggs (optional)
275ml/10 fl oz milk
Butter for roasting tin
2 bay leaves

Small finely sliced onion
6 crushed peppercorns
3/4 cloves
Sauce
30g/1oz butter
30g/1oz flour
45ml/3tbsp cream
2 tbsp chopped parsley

Topping
500g/1 lb creamy mashed potato
30g/1 oz butter

Salt and pepper

Lay the coley and smoked haddock in a buttered roasting or ovenproof dish. Scatter the sliced onion, crushed peppercorns and cloves. Season with a little salt. Pour the milk over. Cover with foil and cook in a moderate oven 180C/350F Gas 4 for 30 minutes.

Remove the fish with a fish slice or spatula onto a plate. Pour the liquid through a sieve to use in the sauce. When the fish is cool enough to handle, flake it off the skin. Put it back into the dish it was cooked in or into a buttered pie dish taking care not to break the flakes too much. Scatter the peeled cooked prawns over.

If using hard boiled eggs, chop them and add.

Melt the butter in a saucepan, stir in the flour and mix. Away from the heat, slowly add the seasoned milk, stirring all the time to prevent lumpiness. Return to a gentle heat and slowly bring to the boil. Add more milk or water to make the sauce smooth and creamy, finally add the parsley.

Remove from heat, add the cream (optional). Taste for seasoning and pour over the fish.

Place the mashed potato in dollops over the fish and with a fork gently spread to cover the surface. Dot with butter.

If it is to be served straight away. Put in a hot oven 230C/450F Gas 8 for 15/20 minutes until thoroughly heated through and golden brown.

If heating from cold. Cook in a moderate oven 180C/350F Gas 4 for 25/30 minutes until golden brown and bubbling.

If you prefer, you needn't cover the fish with mashed potato but with breadcrumbs and grated cheddar cheese. Cook or grill till bubbling and golden.

Oriental Coley with Quick Bean Sprouts

Serves 4
1kg/2lbs coley
2 tbsp soy sauce
Juice a half a lemon or lime
1 tbsp grated fresh ginger
2 tbsp chopped coriander

2 tbsp chopped chives
2 finely chopped cloves garlic
1 red chilli, finely sliced, seeds removed
1 sliced red or green pepper
1tbsp sesame oil
Salt and pepper

Take the fish and with a sharp knife, start at one end removing the flesh from the skin. Cut into bite sized pieces.

Place in a bowl. Add the soy sauce, lemon or lime juice, grated ginger, coriander and chives. Season with salt and pepper. Leave to marinate for 1 hour or until needed.

In a wok or frying pan, gently fry the chopped garlic and onion in the sesame oil. Add the finely sliced pepper and chilli, having removed the seeds. Cook for five minutes constantly turning. Add the coley and other ingredients turning gently with a wooden spatula until cooked through, about five minutes.

Serve with boiled rice or noodles and stir-fried vegetables of your choice, for example:

Quick Bean Sprouts
1 carton (250 g/8 oz) bean sprouts
Small piece fresh ginger
1 fat clove chopped garlic

1 tbsp soy sauce
3 or 4 spring onions
1 tbsp corn or groundnut oil

Wash and drain the bean sprouts.

Gently fry the garlic and sliced spring onions in the oil. Add the bean sprouts, chopped ginger and soy sauce. Cook for 2 to 3 minutes, turning all the time.

Various additions can be made such as finely sliced mushrooms or water chestnuts.

CONGER EEL

Conger Eel	*Conger conger*
Guernsey French	*congre* (m), *caongre* (m), *anguelle* (f)
Jersey French	*andeguille* (f), *congre* (m)
French	*congre* (m)

The conger has long associations with the islands. During medieval times conger and other fish were salted and dried and exported as far as Gascony in south-west France. It was an important source of wealth.

The island was divided into Fiefs or Estates, each one headed by a Seigneur or Lord. He owned the places where the fish was dried and salted. He provided the racks for salting and drying it, charging a tax for their use. Conger continued to be exported until the end of the 16th century.

Conger has a smooth, scaleless, serpent-like body. Its upper jaw is longer than its lower. It has a dorsal fin which runs almost the whole length of its body while the ventral fin runs from half way along. Its colour varies but it is usually dark grey or brown with grey sides and a light gold or white belly. The flesh is white. It is available all year round but best during the summer months. It can grow up to 180 cms. The best size for cooking is 8 kilos/ 16lbs. They were caught in willow pots but now wire ones are used. They are also caught with lines.

A friend was telling me he used to enjoy skin-diving for conger with an underwater harpoon gun. If he saw a pair of cold steely eyes looking at him from a crevice, he would circle the rocks to see where the tail was. If it encircled the rocks, he would leave it alone! A fight with a conger would be dangerous and exhausting. Congers are popular with anglers but very strong tackle is needed and plenty of patience as there will invariably be a long tussle.

Congers are very common around our waters and there are many stories about them. They live in rocky crevices, in holes in sea walls, old wrecks and harbour jetties.

The conger and octopus were vividly brought to life by Victor Hugo in *Toilers of the Sea*. So much so that I used to be terrified swimming down at Portelet at Pleinmont in the inner jetty in case a conger should be lurking – viciously strong jaws waiting for a juicy foot!

In fact the conger isn't normally aggressive. Only when it senses danger does it react. It is so strong that if caught in a pot, it can thrash around eventually breaking it. Even on board they can be dangerous, biting through a man's boot with ease.

The conger and the lobster often share the same hole because octopus prey on lobster and conger prey on octopus. This was in days gone by as we rarely see an octopus in these waters any longer.

The conger eel has white flesh which is covered with a thick gelatinous skin.

It is also a very bony fish, so care must be taken over which cut to use. The cut from just behind the head to under the vent is the best one. Chunks of conger can be egg and bread crumbed or battered and fried – passing as poor man's scampi.

Conger used to be a very important fish with islanders as it was a cheap source of nourishing food.

Mr. Nichols tells me that his Grandmother would slit a conger eel down the middle, and, having heavily salted and peppered it, hang it on the washing line to dry. It would be brought in as the sun began to set so that it wouldn't be affected by any humidity in the air. The next day it would be hung out again until it had become as dry as a board. It was then stored near the kitchen range

When it was needed, it would be soaked for 36 hours, with several changes of water before it was cooked. By then it would have plumped up to look almost like a fresh piece.

~   ~   ~

Baked Conger

Serves 4

Take the whole middle cut 2kg/4lbs

60g/2oz butter	1 teasp. chopped thyme
275ml /10 fl oz dry cider	Finely grated rind & juice of 1 lemon
Forcemeat stuffing	1 egg
180g/6oz fresh breadcrumbs	30g/1oz butter
3tbsp chopped parsley	Salt and pepper

Mix together the breadcrumbs, seasoning and herbs. Bind with lemon juice, beaten egg and 30g/ 1 oz of melted butter.

Carefully clean the conger and remove any blood and loose bones.

With a sharp knife make a deep cut either side of the dorsal fin down to the central bone, continue the whole length of the piece and then ease the fin out. Turn over and cut the flesh along the bone to make room for the stuffing.

Rinse and dry, sprinkle with salt. Push into shape and stuff with the forcemeat and tie securely. If the stuffing looks as if it is going to escape, a halved cooking apple pushed in at each end will act as a plug and goes well with the cider too.

Put in a buttered roasting tin and place a few dots of butter where the fin was. Baste with cider. Lightly cover with foil, not tightly otherwise the conger will be steamed. The foil prevents your oven becoming very messy as this dish tends to splutter.

Bake in a hot oven 220C/425F Gas 7 for an hour, lowering the heat to 190C/375F Gas 5 after half an hour. Test with a skewer to see if it is done. Cook longer if necessary.

Serve with mashed potato and parsley sauce.

An alternative way of cooking is to finely slice a red cabbage and cooking apple into an earthenware casserole, season and add 4/5 crushed juniper berries, 1 level tbsp brown sugar and the cider.

Place the stuffed conger so that it nestles down into the cabbage/ apple mixture.

Place a good knob of butter where the fin was. Cover with a lid or foil and place in a medium oven to cook for 2 hours. Long slow cooking is necessary for the apple and cabbage to collapse. Serve with boiled potatoes.

Conger Baked in Milk and Saffron

In old Guernsey recipes, saffron was used quite often.

Serves 4
A piece of conger about 2kilos/4lbs, from just behind the head.
60g/2oz butter   Good pinch saffron threads or
60g/2oz flour   1 sachet of powdered saffron
3 or 4 bay leaves   550ml/1pt milk
                                    Salt and pepper

Place the strands of saffron in a teacup. Cover with boiling water and leave to infuse for 30 minutes. Alternatively you can use a sachet of powdered saffron.

Clean and rinse the conger, removing the dorsal fin. Reshape if it doesn't want to stay put and tie with string. It needs to be neat and compact.

Place in an ovenproof dish or roasting tin. Pour over 550ml/1pint of milk, season with salt and pepper and the bay leaves. Cover with foil and cook in a hot oven 220C/425F, Gas 7 for 1 hour.

Check to see that it is done by using a knife, teasing away some of the flesh. If it comes away from the bone, it is done. If it requires longer cooking,

reduce the heat checking to see if it is cooked every 15 minutes.

Strain off the milk and keep the conger warm.

In a saucepan, melt 60g/2oz of butter. Add 60g/2oz flour and mix until well incorporated. Gently add the strained saffron or the sachet of saffron. Add the milk the conger was cooked in. Stir until smooth and creamy, adding more milk if necessary. Check seasoning.

Lift the conger onto a serving dish. Remove the string.

Pour over the sauce and scatter with marigold petals, if you have some at hand.

Serve with boiled potatoes and spring greens or some other colourful vegetable.

Conger Fries

Serves 4
1kilo/2lbs conger
60g/2oz cornmeal. As an alternative use crushed cornflakes or flour
1tsp paprika or pinch cayenne
Juice of 1 lemon
Seasoning
Oil for frying

Remove the meat from the skin and bone, making sure that no bones are left. Cut into sugar lump or goujon pieces. Sprinkle with paprika or cayenne, lemon juice, salt and pepper, leave to marinate for as long as possible as this helps to tenderise the flesh.

Drain. Pat dry in kitchen paper. Roll in crushed cornflakes or cornmeal. Alternatively put the crushed flakes or cornmeal into a paper or plastic bag, add the cubes of conger and gently shake to coat.

Heat the oil until hot but not smoking. Gently lower the pieces in, piece by piece.

Fry 2 to 3 minutes until golden brown.

Alternatively, dip the goujons in batter (cod recipe).

Cutlets of Conger

Serves 4
Choose pieces from just behind the head
4 cutlets 180g/6oz each
Flour for coating
1 onion
750g /1½ lb tomatoes
Handful each of fresh rosemary and thyme
Seasoning
275ml/10fl oz white wine or cider
Oil for frying
60g / 2oz butter
This recipe requires long slow cooking.

Having washed and patted dry the cutlets, toss in flour. Fry them in oil and 30g /1 oz butter until golden brown. Keep warm.

In the same pan, fry the sliced onion and chopped tomatoes in 30g/1 oz butter. Add the chopped rosemary and thyme. Season. Place in an oven-proof dish. Arrange the cutlets on top with a knob of the remaining butter on each.

Pour the cider or wine around plus a little water to make sure there is adequate liquid so that it won't dry out. Cover with a lid or foil and place in a moderate oven325F/170C Gas 3 until bubbling. Turn the heat down as low as possible and leave to simmer for 3 to 4 hours. Make sure there is liquid so that nothing sticks to the bottom of the dish. The tomato and onion mixture should be mushy.

Serve with boiled potatoes. Alternatively, a mixture of boiled diced parsnip and carrot with a dollop of butter added on serving.

Conger Eel Soup

Serves 4

500g/1 lb piece of conger
30g / 1oz butter
500g/1 lb tomatoes
1 leek
1 onion
1 small deseeded chilli
2 carrots

500g/1 lb potatoes
1 tsp paprika
2 bay leaves
Sprigs of fresh or 1 tsp dried thyme
800 ml / $1\frac{1}{2}$ pts stock
Salt and pepper

Wash the conger carefully, removing all traces of blood. Remove the skin and cut the meat into very small pieces removing all the bones. You can make stock from the bits with the addition of a handful of herbs and seasoning by bringing it to the boil and simmering for ten minutes and strain. Alternatively you can use a fish stock cube.

In the rinsed pan, fry the chopped onion, leek and carrots in the butter. Add the chopped potatoes, chopped tomatoes and chopped chilli. Add the stock, bay leaves, thyme and paprika. Season.

Add the conger pieces and allow to simmer for 30/40 minutes.

Remove the bay leaves and two tablespoonfuls of conger meat.

Liquidise but check for bones first. Alternatively sieve or mouli it.

Reheat, check seasoning. Add the reserved bits of conger and on serving a light dusting of paprika.

During summer, marigold petals are scattered over the soup before serving.

GARFISH

Garfish or Longnose	*Belone belone*
Guernsey French	*orfi* or *erfi* (m)
Jersey French	*orfi* (m)
French	*orphie* (m)

Garfish is found throughout the Channel and southern North Sea. It is a seasonal fish so not seen until August, when it is available until November.

Channel Islanders are very fond of it.

Herbert Nichols told me that often in the past communal nets were set in a line, usually in one of the smaller bays, such as Bordeaux. Slivers of dry parsnip were gently laid on the water, being so light there was no noise or splash to frighten off the fish. For some reason the fish were attracted to it. The two ends of the net eventually met having been pulled into a circle by fishermen in two rowing-boats. The nets would be pulled into the boats along with the garfish.

Garfish was once plentiful but is now seen far less. However, they are easily picked out on the fish-mongers slab because of their long streamlined blueish green body and beaky jaws filled with razor sharp teeth - its name means spearfish.

Their bones are blue or green caused by a harmless phosphate of iron. I remember being told that the bones were poisonous which rather puts you off eating the fish, but this is untrue.

Garfish are popular fish with shore anglers.

In days gone by, before refrigeration, garfish would be gutted and salted and spread out to dry to be used during the lean winter months.

The best size is up to 60 cms/24 inches

When buying garfish bear in mind how many pieces you will cut from it. For each portion you will need a piece approx 15cms/6in long.

Fried Garfish

This is a simple way of cooking garfish. Rinse and pat dry. Coat in seasoned flour and gently fry in half oil, half butter. Serve with wedges of lemon.

Braised Garfish

Serves 4
4 pieces each weighing approx 180g / 6 oz or 15 cms/6in
Seasoned flour for coating
About 2 tbsp olive oil
1 onion
3-4 cloves garlic
2 tbsp chopped parsley
150ml/5fl oz. white wine or water

Fry the sliced onion in a little of the oil, add the chopped garlic and fry until beginning to turn golden. Place in an oven-proof dish. Fry the floured garfish in the remaining oil. Arrange on the onions, pour the white wine or water around, sprinkle with chopped parsley. Season. Cover with foil and cook in a moderately hot oven 190C/375F Gas 5 for 20/30minutes.
Serve with wedges of lemon.

A bowl of mushy peas would go well. Another bowl of mashed or boiled potatoes too.

GREY MULLET

Grey Mullet	*Crenimugil labrosus* (thick-lipped)
Guernsey French	*gris molet* (m)
Jersey French	*ouothillard* (m)
French	*muge* or *mulet* (m)

Grey Mullet is available all year round.

A heavily scaled fish with a dark greeny grey back and silvery sides but with darker grey bands running the whole length of the body. It has a pronounced upper lip.

If caught in muddy estuaries it tends to have a muddy flavour but that doesn't apply to our waters. Because it comes inshore, it also has the reputation of being a scavenger but this is untrue as it feeds on planktonic organisms.

It is a popular fish with anglers as it likes to stay close to the coast.

The flesh tends to be soft so it is best to cook it whole. If left to get cold, this allows the flesh to firm up. It is a good fish for barbecues

The soft roe is the one used in the making of taramasalata, the creamy pale pink paté popular in Greece and Turkey.

~   ~   ~

Baked or Grilled Grey Mullet

Serves 4
4 whole mullet each weighing approx. 360g/12oz
4 bay leaves
Olive oil
Juice of 1 lemon
1 level tbsp chopped lemon thyme
Salt and pepper

Gut and scale the fish. Pat dry. Slash the body diagonally on both sides 2 or 3 times.

Oil a baking tray or grill pan. Lay the fish side by side, season with salt and ground black pepper. Sprinkle with lemon juice making sure it goes into the slashes. Sprinkle with chopped thyme and place a bay leaf on each mullet.   Drizzle olive oil over.

Place in a hot oven 220C/425F Gas 7 for 15 minutes, longer if using bigger fish.

If grilling, place under a hot grill cooking for 7 minutes each side.

Once again if using bigger fish, grill a little longer.

Serve with braised sliced potatoes and onion, milk and cream, better known as Pommes Anna. Don't overcook so that they become dry, creaminess is important.

A tossed green salad too, to freshen the palate.

The mullet can be cooked as above and allowed to cool and then served with mayonnaise which has plenty of lemon juice added. Mullet firms up beautifully when cold.

Grey Mullet with Baked Aubergines

Mullet can take stronger tasting vegetables which would overpower fish such as plaice. This recipe is best served cold.

Serves 4

4 mullet each approx. 340g/12oz	2 shallots
Juice of 1 lemon, olive oil, seasoning	2 heaped tbsps
Baked Aubergines	chopped parsley
3 aubergines	2 cloves garlic
6 tomatoes	Salt and pepper
4 tbsp white breadcrumbs	Ground coriander and cumin

The aubergines can be baked the day before, the flavours developing overnight.

Slice the aubergines and sprinkle with salt, this draws out the watery bitterness. Leave for approx 10 minutes. Rinse under running water, pat dry with kitchen paper.

Oil an ovenproof dish and layer with aubergine, finely chopped shallot, garlic and chopped tomatoes. Now a dusting of ground cumin and coriander, salt and pepper.

Next, a layer of breadcrumbs mixed with parsley. Repeat with another layer of aubergines, spices and then breadcrumbs.

Drizzle with olive oil and 2/3tbsp water.   Cover with a lid or foil.

Bake in a moderate oven for 1 hour. Leave to cool until needed.

Cook the mullet well in advance

Make a couple of slashes on the sides of the cleaned mullet and place in an oiled roasting tin. Season and sprinkle with lemon juice and olive oil.

Bake in a hot oven for 15/20 minutes, or cook under a hot grill.

Allow to cool.

Serve with the aubergines and an aioli or similar sauce.

Don't take the aubergines straight from the refrigerator. I find they taste better served at room temperature.

GURNARD

Gurnard	*Triglidae*
There are four gurnard found in our water but the	
Red is the most common	
Guernsey French	*grounnard* (m)
Jersey French	*gronnard* (m)
French	*grondin rouge* (m)

The red gurnard is easy to recognise because of its large bony head, spiny dorsal fin, tapering body and spiny gill covers. Because of its fins and gill covers, it looks as if it could take off, rather like a flying-fish! It is underrated because of its big head and all those fins.

Don't be put off by its unusual appearance as the flesh is white and firm.

It is good for poaching, frying and baking. It can be filleted or cooked whole and is excellent for fish soups.

Because it gets passed by, it is comparatively cheap.

It is a popular fish with anglers.

Gurnard live on the sandy seabed where they are said to grunt to each other! My raconteur, Herbert Nichols tells me that a group of them grunting away on the seabed can be heard by fishermen sitting in their boats above!

It is available all year but should be scaled straight away to keep its colour.

Baked Gurnard

Serves 4
Two Red Gurnard totalling approx. 1½ kilo/3 lbs
Juice of 1 lemon
1 kilo/2lbs tomatoes   4 rashers streaky bacon
1 clove garlic   Salt and pepper
3 or 4 shallots   Chopped chives

Gut and clean the gurnard, pat dry. If you don't like the look of that bony head, cut it off. Finely slice the tomatoes into an ovenproof casserole. Add the chopped garlic and chopped shallots. Lay the gurnard on top, season and sprinkle with the lemon juice, cover with foil and bake for 30/40 minutes in a moderate oven.

While cooking, fry or grill the bacon till crisp.

Before serving, let the gurnard relax for 10 minutes

On serving scatter with crumbled bacon and scissored chives.

Fillets of Gurnard with Ratatouille

Serves 4
8 fillets approximately 90g/3 oz each   500g/1lb tomatoes
Flour for coating and seasoning   250g/8oz onion
Oil and a little butter for frying   Fat clove garlic
Ratatouille   Olive oil
1 aubergine   Seasoning
2 green peppers   1 heaped tbsp chopped parsley
500g/1lb courgettes   3-4 sage leaves (optional)

Slice the aubergine, sprinkle with salt and leave for 10 minutes to draw the bitter juice. Rinse, pat dry, turn and repeat. Pat dry. Fry the slices in olive oil and put to one side. Next fry the sliced courgettes, put to one side.

Now fry the sliced onion and peppers until they collapse, add the crushed garlic and season. Add the chopped tomatoes and cook all together until soft and most of the juice has evaporated.

In an ovenproof casserole, place the fried aubergine and courgettes. Sprinkle with parsley and scissored sage then add the onion, pepper and tomato mixture. Season.

Gently stir the mixture so that all the vegetables become incorporated. Cover and cook for 30 minutes. Uncover and cook a little longer until most of the juice has evaporated.

Leave to cool.

Ratatouille happily reheats.

Coat the fillets of gurnard with seasoned flour. Fry in oil and a little butter, about 4 minutes each side.

Serve with wedges of lemon, the ratatouille and lots of bread.

A whole gurnard baked in the oven with herbs and a little oil and allowed to get cold is excellent. Serve it with mayonnaise and potato salad and any other salad of your choice.

HADDOCK

Haddock	*Melanogrammus aeglefinus*
Guernsey French	*églefin* (m)
Jersey French	*l'héthique* (f)
French	*aiglefin* (m) or *églefin* (m)

A fish growing up to 75cm/30 inches. It has three dorsal fins and two ventral fins on the underside with pelvic fins under the throat. It also has a small chin barbel but what makes it easier to recognise is the black spot or thumb-print on the side of the body at the front of the lateral line behind the gills. It has a dark grey back and silvery underside. It is uncommon in these waters. It is imported as fillets from the UK and is sold fresh or smoked.

Genuine smoked haddock is also known as Arbroath smokies (hot smoked) or Finnan Haddie (cold smoked). Cold smoked is expensive. Dyed smoked haddock is cheaper but the flavour is not so good. It is definitely worth paying that little bit extra for real smoked haddock as opposed to dyed.

Baked Haddock Pie

Serves 4

1,250g /2$\frac{1}{2}$ lbs fish made up of 750g /1$\frac{1}{2}$ lbs fresh haddock and 500g/1lb smoked

Butter for greasing the ovenproof dish

250g/8oz mushrooms

90g/3oz butter

1 tbsp chopped parsley

3275l/10 fl. oz. creamy milk

30g/1oz plain flour

2/3 bay leaves

750g/1$\frac{1}{2}$ lbs potatoes

Salt and pepper

Place the fish in a buttered ovenproof dish. Season and add the bay leaves and milk.

Cover with foil and bake in a moderate oven for 20 minutes.

Meanwhile cook the sliced mushrooms in 30g/1oz butter till the juice runs.

Make the sauce by melting the remaining butter and adding the flour to make a roux.

When the fish is cooked, add the cooking liquid to the sauce, adding a little extra milk if the sauce is too thick. Finally, add the parsley and check for seasoning.

In the same dish, flake the haddock, adding the mushrooms.

Pour over the sauce and cover with mashed potato.

Dot with a little butter and place in the oven until bubbling.

This is a very comforting dish.

Haddock with Tomato Sauce

Serves 4

4 fillets of unsmoked haddock each weighing approx.180g/6oz

Seasoned flour for coating

Sauce

500g/1 lb tomatoes or 1 tin (400g)chopped tomatoes

1 medium finely chopped onion,

1 fat clove chopped garlic

1tbsp olive oil

60g/2oz butter

2/3 bay leaves

1 tsp lemon thyme

Dash of tabasco

Salt and pepper

Juice of half a lemon

It really is worth the trouble making fresh tomato sauce as it tastes so good. Fortunately, one thing that is plentiful in the islands during the summer months is tomatoes.

In a small heavy-duty casserole or a saucepan, fry the chopped onion and garlic in olive oil.

Add the tomatoes, bay leaf, a splash of tabasco and lemon thyme.

Make sure the mixture is covered with water. Simmer gently on top or in a moderate oven for at least 30/40mins, adding more water if necessary.

Remove the bay leaf and sieve or mouli the pulp – you will be left with nothing but a few tomato skins.

Fry the flour-coated fillets in butter till golden brown.

Serve with the sauce and a mixture of rice and courgettes or peas.

Kedgeree

Our very first overseas posting was Bombay and we had the luxury of a cook. He came from Madras so served everything hot. Over the years his dishes had mellowed to suit our western taste. His kedgeree was a mound of golden saffron-infused rice with flakes of fish. Often golden-yellow lentils or dhall were included. The mound was encircled by a ring of the sieved white of hard- boiled eggs and another of the yolks – never the twain were mixed. Just before serving his final flourish was a scattering of a handful of slivered almonds and plumped up sultanas over the golden mountain.

Our Cook would use pomfret (a local fish) but we have to adapt the dish. I think using smoked haddock is the best but other flaky fish is suitable.

Serves 4

750g/1½ lb smoked haddock
250g / 8oz Basmati rice
Good pinch of saffron strands
(if you don't have saffron,
    use half tsp tumeric)
1 onion
2 tbsp sunflower oil (or similar)

1 tsp hot Madras curry powder
2 tbsp sultanas
1 tbsp slivered toasted almonds
2 hard boiled eggs
60g/2 oz butter
Salt and pepper

First method

Place the strands of saffron in a teacup and cover with boiling water, leave to infuse. (If you prefer, pound the saffron strands in a pestle and add with the rice).

Place the haddock in a roasting tin and cover with water, making sure it is skin side up. Place in a moderate oven 190C/375F Gas 5 for 15-20 minutes. Put to one side until cool enough to handle.

In an ovenproof casserole or heavy duty pan, lightly fry the finely chopped onion in the oil. Add the Basmati rice turning for a minute, then the curry powder (increase the amount if you like a hotter dish), and finally the saffron water. If you are using turmeric or pounded saffron, add it now. Just cover the rice with water then cover with foil or a lid. Cook in a moderate oven for 30-40mins. Check that all the liquid has been absorbed. Dot the rice generously with butter and gently turn. If the bottom seems stuck, do not worry, put to one side, it soon relaxes and loosens its grip.

Carefully flake the haddock. Add to the rice gently turning to distribute it.

Second method: Boiling the rice

Put the saffron threads in a small cup and cover with boiling water. Leave to infuse for 15 minutes. Boil the rice for 9 minutes. Drain, add the saffron water. Stir in a generous knob of butter. Cover.

Fry the finely chopped onion (while the rice is boiling). When soft add the curry powder.

Place the rice in a large ovenproof dish, add the flaked haddock and curried onion. Gently turn until the fish is well incorporated. Cover to keep warm.

To serve both methods:

In a little oil or butter, gently fry the slivered almonds and sultanas until plumped up.

Either serve in the dish it was cooked in, or turn onto a flat dish or plate. Form it into a mound. Another way is to put the cooked rice, curried onion and fish into a pudding basin, press firmly to compact it. Place a plate on top and invert it so that it comes out like a plum pudding. It can then be garnished on top and around.

Garnish whichever way you have cooked it with the sieved egg, (roughly chopped is just as colourful), sprinkle with the almonds and sultanas.

All manner of chutneys and pickles can be served, especially the lime ones.

Wedges of lemon or lime sharpen the flavour and help moisten it.

Haddock Soufflé

Serves 4
I find that it is not really necessary to cook a soufflé in a soufflé dish. Any ovenproof dish is just as good.
375g/12oz smoked haddock
4 eggs
275ml/10fl oz milk
30g/1oz flour
30g/1oz butter
1 tsp dry mustard
1 tbsp chopped parsley
Salt and cayenne
2 bay leaves

Place the haddock in an ovenproof dish. Add the milk and bay leaves. Cover and cook gently for approximately 20/30 mins in a moderate to hot oven, until tender and easy to flake. Remove from milk and keep warm. In a saucepan melt the butter. Add the flour and mustard powder. Gently add the milk, stirring till smooth over a very low heat. Cook until thickened and smooth, adding a little more milk if necessary to obtain a creamy sauce. Remove from the heat.

Add the egg yolks one by one stirring all the time. Season with salt and cayenne.

Remove haddock flakes from the skin, gently breaking them into small pieces (if you prefer a smoother texture mash the flakes), add them to the sauce.

Whisk the egg whites until stiff. Gently fold into mixture and turn into a well buttered soufflé or ovenproof dish.

Bake in a hot oven 220C/425F Gas 7 for 20 minutes. This will give a crispy crust with soft inside.

This is also an ideal picnic dish when cold. Cut into wedges with a salad, it really is very good.

HAKE

Hake	*Merluccius merluccius*
Jersey French	*mèrluche* (f)
French	*merlu* (m)

This is a distant cousin of the cod. It grows up to 1 metre. Hake is not found in these waters but is caught off the west coast of Ireland.

Not an attractive fish on the fishmonger's slab and usually bypassed. Its back is grey/blue becoming lighter on the sides and belly. It has a large mouth which is black inside and it has hinged teeth. It is available all year round and is sold whole, as steaks or in fillets.

Hake was once popular, then demand dropped but it is now enjoying a revival. People have realised that it is a very good fish to eat. It is firm and stays that way. It doesn't shrink even after a longish cooking in the oven.

In the past it was used for fish pies, fish cakes etc., where a plentiful fish with little demand could be used.

Baked Hake with Cider and Tomatoes

Serves 4
4 hake steaks each weighing 180g/6 oz to 250g/8 oz
1 kilo/2 lbs tomatoes

2 cloves garlic	275ml/10 fl oz dry cider
2 small or 1 large onion	2 tbsp olive oil
1 tsp chopped thyme	30g / 1oz butter
4 bay leaves	Salt and pepper

Chop the onion and garlic and fry in the olive oil until soft, add the roughly chopped tomatoes and thyme. Season with salt and black pepper, then add the cider. Stir and allow to bubble gently till soft and mushy until most of the liquid has evaporated.

Place in an ovenproof dish, with the hake steaks on top, drizzle a little olive oil and place a bay leaf on each. Cover with foil and bake in a fairly hot oven 190C/375F Gas 5 for 20-25 minutes. Dot with butter. Cook for a further 10 minutes uncovered.

Serve with mashed or new potatoes and a green vegetable, such as creamed spinach.

Grilled or Fried Hake with a Spinach and Leek Sauce

Serves 4

4 fillets of hake each weighing 180g/6 oz to 250g/8 oz

For the sauce	3 tbsp double cream
30g/1oz flour	Grated nutmeg
30g/1oz butter	1 tbsp oil and knob of butter for frying
500g/1 lb spinach	30g/1 oz butter
2 small or 1 large leek	Salt and pepper

In a saucepan place the washed, roughly torn spinach and the finely sliced leek, season with salt and pepper. Add a little water. Simmer gently till collapsed, about 5 minutes. Drain, reserving the water.

Whizz the spinach and leek in the food processor.

Melt the butter in a saucepan and add the flour to make a roux. Gently add a little of the spinach and leek water, not too much as you need a thick consistency. Mix until smooth, bring to the boil, adjust seasoning if necessary, adding a grating of nutmeg. Add the blended vegetables, stirring until you have a smooth creamy sauce, adding a little more of the vegetable water if necessary.

Wash and pat dry the hake fillets. Coat with flour and gently fry in half butter and oil.

If grilling, it is unnecessary to flour them, just lay in the grill pan, sprinkle with salt, pepper and place a knob of butter on each. Grill for 3 minutes on each side. Keep warm while you quickly bring the sauce to the boil. Remove from heat, add the cream and serve either poured over the fish or separately.

Goes well with boiled brown or basmati rice to which you have added 1 tbsp chopped parsley and a generous dollop of butter.

HALIBUT

Atlantic Halibut	*Hippoglossus hippoglossus*
Guernsey French	*halibot* (m)
Jersey French	*halibot* (m), *fiêtan* (m)
French	*flétan* (m)

An extremely large flatfish, weighing up to 300kg and 2.5m in length. The upper side is a deep tan with shades of olive green, while the underside is white. Halibut are not found in these waters. They are found on the fishing banks in the North Atlantic and on the sandy banks between Scotland and Norway. They are best during the spring.

It is sold as cutlets, steaks and fillets. Its white flaky flesh is much in demand and commands a high price. (Many halibut sold in Guernsey are imported from Canada and can be Pacific halibut).

The oil from the liver is rich in nutrients.

Grilled Halibut Steaks with Four Herbs Sauce

Serves 4
4 steaks 180g/6oz each
Olive oil
Salt and pepper

Brush the steaks with olive oil and place in an oiled grill pan. Season with salt and ground black pepper. Cook under a moderate grill for 6-7 minutes on each side.

Sauce
30g/1oz flour
30g/1oz butter
150ml/5fl oz dry white wine
3 tbsp double cream
1 tbsp chopped parsley
1 tbsp chopped chives
1 tbsp chopped chervil
1 tsp chopped thyme
Salt and pepper

While grilling the fish, make the sauce.

Melt the butter, add the flour and stir until smooth. Gently add the wine, bring to the boil, perhaps a little more wine or water if too thick. Add the chopped herbs and season. If any juices have run from the fish add these to the sauce, finally the cream. Heat almost to boiling point. Aim for a rich green creamy sauce, the greener the better as it looks really good against the white flesh of the halibut.

Grilled Halibut with Spinach

Serves 4
4 steaks or cutlets each weighing 180g/6oz
750g/ 1$\frac{1}{2}$ lb fresh spinach
2 medium onions
90g/3oz butter
Nutmeg
Salt
Cayenne pepper
2 tbsp double cream
Juice of half lemon + 4 wedges

Grill in the same way as the previous recipe.

Finely slice the onions and fry in half the butter, add a little water and cook slowly until soft, brown and transparent, season with salt and cayenne pepper. The onions should be dryish so that you can serve them in little mounds.

Boil the spinach until it collapses, roughly chop in a colander, return to the saucepan, season, stir in the cream, the grated nutmeg and lemon juice.

Serve each steak or cutlet on a small bed of spinach with a pile of onions alongside. Garnish with a wedge of lemon.

A dish of creamy mashed potato dusted with a grating of nutmeg is all that is needed.

Rough Puff Pastry Parcels of Halibut

Recently I thought I would try making Eccles Cakes. The recipe said Rough Puff and my immediate reaction was to go to the shop for some Puff Pastry. On second thoughts, I decided to make some. I discovered it was very easy, the thought of rolling and re-rolling and re-rolling yet again was pure imagination as it is very simple.

I realise I digress but it is worth the trouble of making pastry for this dish. Halibut is a special occasion fish so merits making an effort!

Serves 4
4 halibut steaks approx 120g/4 oz
1 tbsp chopped capers
1 tbsp chopped green olives
1 tbsp chopped parsley
1 tbsp snipped chives
1 tbsp lemon juice
1 tbsp olive oil
1 egg
Salt and pepper

Rough Puff Pastry
250g/8 oz plain flour
180g/6oz butter
Water
Pinch salt

Cut the butter into four equal pieces. Chop each quarter into smaller pieces.

Mix one quarter with flour and salt so that it remains lumpy and not fine like breadcrumbs. Mix with very cold water to a firm, slightly sticky dough.

Knead into an oblong shape and roll fairly thin. Dot the top two-thirds with the second quarter of butter. Fold the unbuttered piece up over half the buttered pastry and fold the top half down, sandwiching the unbuttered piece. Turn, sealing the edges with the rolling pin and gently roll to the same oblong shape as before.

Repeat with the last two quarters of butter. With all the butter safely in, roll once more, fold as before.

Rest (the pastry) till needed in the refrigerator. Give it at least an hour.

In a bowl mix the olive oil, parsley, green olives, lemon juice, capers, snipped chives, salt and pepper.

When ready, roll the pastry into a square and divide into four equal pieces. Each piece needs to be approximately 15 cms/ 6 inches square, making sure it is big enough to hold the fish with plenty of pastry around.

Divide the olive mixture into 4 and place a little pile on each piece of pastry.

Having removed all bones and shaped the fish into a circle, place it on top of the mixture, pressing down. Moisten around the edge, draw up and pinch together. Turn over and gently flatten, brush with beaten egg.

Make a small hole for the steam to escape. Decorate with leaves from the pastry trimmings. Bake in a hot oven 220C/425F Gas 7 for 30-40 minutes.

Check, as they may need a little longer. Aim for a sizzling hot golden parcel.

A hollandaise or really green parsley sauce goes well.

Serve with finely sliced tomatoes with chopped chives and torn basil leaves or a dressed mixed green salad and a lemony vinaigrette.

HERRING

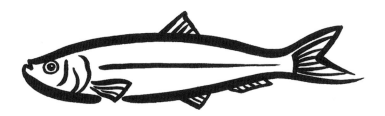

Herring	*Clupea harengus*
Guernsey French	*heran, herron* or *herrang* (m)
Jersey French	*héthan* (m)
French	*hareng* (m)

A sad note from *The People of the Sea* by A.G .Jamieson tells us that the herring had been found around Guernsey until 1830 but in that year disappeared. According to local tradition, this change occurred because some Guernseyman committed the sin of fishing on Sunday!

Herrings are a fish from northern seas. Its name means 'army' because of the vast shoals it travels in. The herring brought wealth to Scotland and the west coast of England. When the herring was in season, girls would arrive in readiness to clean and salt them. No one thought they would ever become scarce because of their vast numbers. Unfortunately, the efficiency of trawlers changed all that, so much so, that herring fishing was banned for several years. Once again they are becoming available.

Some herrings are still caught in local waters but most are imported.

A slender scaly fish, silvery in colour but darker blue on the back. It grows up to about 40cms/ 16inches and is available all year round though not so common in the spring as this is the spawning time. Young herrings are sold as whitebait.

Other members of the family which have been treated by either pickling, smoking, salting or brining are Yarmouth Bloaters, Kippers, Buckling and even Red Herrings!

On the fishmonger's slab a fresh herring looks a robust fish but in fact has to be handled very carefully.

Fresh herrings seem to marry very happily with mustard, oatmeal, gooseberries, rhubarb and sorrel, apple and horseradish. Tart flavours go particularly well with them.

Red Herrings (of the fishy variety, at least!) have all but disappeared. They were salted in barrels, complete with gut, then smoked very slowly over slow-burning fires until they took on a red glow. The slowness of the smoking made them tough and able to stand changes of temperature and humidity without going rotten. They could then be exported as far away as Nigeria. With improved transportation and refrigeration, demand for the Red Herring decreased. Also methods of curing improved so that the Red Herring gave way to the Kipper.

Kippers are herrings which are briefly salted and then smoked.

The herring is slit open and flattened, to resemble a kite. It is then hung by its tail.

The colour depends on the length of time in the smokehouse. It varies from a light rust to a deep mahogany.

Bloaters remain ungutted. They are lightly salted and then smoked for about 12 hours. They won't keep long because the gut has begun to ferment resulting in the roundness of the belly, hence the name 'bloater'. There is a certain earthiness about bloaters and although the flavour of the flesh is delicate the taste of the gut seems to invade the whole fish. Bloater Paste is another well known name from the past and still available.

Yarmouth Bloaters are not a commom sight on the fishmonger's slab here in Guernsey but are available now and again.

They can be grilled and served with wedges of lemon and bread and butter.

I poach them in water for 20 minutes.

My husband loves them but once a year is enough for me!

Grilled, Fried or Baked Herrings

Serves 4
4 herrings each weighing approx. 240g/8oz
1 level tbsp dry mustard   Seasoning
120g/4oz fine or medium oatmeal   Sunflower oil

Mix the mustard, oatmeal and seasoning.

Brush each fish with a little oil. Roll the oiled fish in the oatmeal, pressing it on.

Lay the fish on an oiled grill pan, frying pan or baking tray. Cook under a hot grill or fry for 4 minutes on each side, or in a hot oven for 15/20 minutes turning once.

Serve with wedges of lemon or with mustard, rhubarb or gooseberry sauce.

Mustard Sauce
Melt 30g/1oz butter, add 30g/1oz flour and 2 tsp dry mustard. Mix well then add 250ml/ 8 fl oz milk. Mix until smooth. Heat to boiling point. Season.

Remove from the heat, and stir in 1 tbsp cream and 1tbsp tarragon vinegar. Serve.

Rhubarb or Gooseberry Sauce
The sauce is made in the same way with both fruits. It is more of a fruit purée than a sauce.

Cut 500g/1lb rhubarb into short pieces. Grate 1 tsp fresh root ginger. Cook both gently with a little water, to prevent sticking, until the juices run. Once the fruit has collapsed and is juicy, sieve. Return to the pan, add 1 tbsp sugar and boil until thick stirring all the time. Remove from the heat and stir in 2 tbsp of double cream. If you prefer a rougher sauce then omit sieving it.
If using gooseberries, top and tail them and cook in the same way. Sieve or mouli them. Add the sugar and the cream.

If you prefer a really tart sauce reduce the amount of sugar or leave it out.

Soused Herrings

Serves 4

4 herrings each weighing approximately 240g/8oz
150 ml/ 5 fl oz malt vinegar (1 small cup)
150 ml/ 5 fl oz water (1small cup)
1 coffee cup of granulated sugar
4 bay leaves
1 tsp crushed black peppercorns
6 cloves
6 crushed cardamom pods
small stick cinnamon
1 small onion

Clean and gut the fish, cutting off the heads. Butterfly bone the herrings by opening down to the tail. Lay them, belly down and, with the palm of the hand, press down. You will feel the bones being released. Turn the fish over, remove the bone and as many little bones as possible that have been left behind. Alternatively, the fish can be filleted.

Place the fish in an ovenproof dish, lay a bay leaf on each.

In a saucepan put the sugar, malt vinegar and water. Add the finely sliced onion and spices. Gently bring to the boil and simmer for 10 minutes. Pour over the fish. Cover with foil and cook in a moderate oven for half an hour. Check to make sure they are quite cooked.

Leave to cool in the vinegar, preferably overnight as this gives the herrings a chance to absorb the flavour of the spices.

Serve with brown bread and butter.

Horseradish or a Mustard Sauce go well with the soused herrings.

Refrigerated, they will keep for up to one week.

Barbecued Stuffed Herrings

Take 4 herrings, 240g/8 oz each
Gut and scale them. Butterfly bone as explained for the previous recipe.

Stuffing

60g/2 oz breadcrumbs	1 tsp chopped green or purple sage
Finely grated rind and juice of 1 lemon	1 egg yolk
1 tbsp chopped capers	Seasoning

Mix the dry ingredients together. Add half the lemon juice and egg yolk to bind.

Divide into 4 portions and roll each one into a sausage shape. Place a 'sausage' along the centre of each boned herring. Close the fish, reshaping it. Tie with raffia or string.

If you have some bay leaves or sprigs of rosemary available, lay them on the skin before tying up the fish.

To keep them intact, you might find it reassuring to cook them in a hinged specialised rack, though this isn't really necessary. Barbecue on a gentle heat.

Alternatively, wrap them in foil and barbecue.

On serving, drizzle the remaining lemon juice over them. If cooked in foil, open the foil and drizzle the lemon juice over.

A good sauce is horseradish:

2 tbsp horseradish sauce	2 tbsp chopped parsley
150ml / 5 fl oz crème fraîche	Tabasco
3 or 4 gherkins depending on size	Salt and pepper

Mix all together having first chopped the gherkins finely. Chill and serve.

Herring Roe

The soft herring roes from the male are known as milt and come as a pair. The hard roes are the eggs and spawn found in the female.

Both can be dipped in egg and rolled in breadcrumbs and then fried in butter.

HUSS, DOGFISH, ROCK SALMON, FLAKE OR RIGG

Lesser spotted catshark	*Scyliorhinus canicula*
Greater spotted catshark	*Scyliorhinus stellaris*
Guernsey French	*tchen-rousse*(m), *roussaenne(f)*, *brochet* (m)
Jersey French	*tchian d'mé* (m), *rousse* (f), *rousset* (m)
French	*rousette* (f), *chien de mer* or *cagnot* (m)

Looking at the various names is confusing as all are used. All relate to the two species which are small sharks. The smaller species grow to about 75 cm long. The larger dogfish can grow to 190 cm.

They are sandy brown with darker spots on the top. The sides shade to a creamy underneath. The mouth is underneath the snout with rows of razor-sharp pointed teeth. Like its bigger cousins, it is a ferocious eater and hunts mackerel and herring. The females lay their eggs in horny egg-cases known as 'mermaids' purses' which they attach to seaweed. Once the babies have hatched, the cases break away and get washed up on the seashore.

There seems to be an automatic rejection of Huss. Is it memories of dissecting it in the school lab? Or is it because it's a member of the shark family? Or is the name dogfish off-putting?

Because of this attitude, it is usually on the fish-monger's slab, skinned and filleted so that it looks like any other white fish. Don't be put off as fresh huss is a better bet than a flabby, tired piece of cod.

It can take strong flavours so is good for currying and happily marries with strong spices such as ginger, cumin and coriander. It can also be used for kebabs as it doesn't fall apart.

It is available all year round.

~   ~   ~

Huss Biriani

Biriani is a spicy (but not hot) dish of Persian origin spread by the Moguls. Biriani is made with Basmati rice, flavoured with saffron and mixed with either meat or fish.

Serves 4

750g/1lb8oz huss
250g/8 oz basmati rice
1 onion
2 cloves garlic
A good pinch of saffron threads or quarter tsp powdered saffron.
Failing saffron, 1 level tsp ground turmeric
1 lb chopped tomatoes or 1 tin tomatoes

1 tbsp ground coriander
1 tbsp ground cumin
5 cms/2 inch piece of cinnamon stick
1 level tsp ground ginger
2 tbsp sunflower oil
Juice of 1 lemon
1 green pepper
Salt and cayenne pepper

Other fish such as cod or pollack can be substituted for huss.

Cut the huss into chunks and sprinkle with ground cumin, coriander, ginger and powdered saffron or tumeric. Add the powdered saffron. If using threads, pound them in a pestle and add to the fish. Season with salt and cayenne and lemon juice.

Leave to marinate for at least 30 minutes.

In a saucepan, frying pan or iron casserole, fry the sliced onion, green pepper and garlic in the oil. Add the chopped tomatoes. When well amalgamated, add the marinated huss along with the cinnamon stick. Add a little water, cover and allow to simmer very slowly, so that it hardly moves for an hour. Alternatively, cook in a moderate oven.

Into a saucepan of boiling salted water, add the basmati rice, cook for 9 minutes.

Strain. Add a knob of butter, cover until needed.

To serve, pile the rice onto a dish, make a hollow and carefully pour in the fish and tomato and pepper mixture.

Mango chutney and lime pickle are good accompaniments to Biriani.

Fried Nuggets of Huss

Serves 4	**Coating Batter**
750g/ 1½ lbs Huss	120g/4 oz flour
2 tsp oil	3 cm/ 1 inch piece of fresh ginger
1 tsp soy sauce	1 egg
1 tsp lemon juice	150 ml/5 fl oz milk and water mixed
Seasoning.	Salt and pepper

Wash, then cut the huss into bite-sized nuggets, roll in kitchen paper to dry.

Mix the oil, soy sauce, grated ginger and lemon juice in a bowl, add the fish. Season with salt and pepper. Thoroughly turn, then leave to marinate.

Make the batter by mixing the flour and egg then gradually the milk/water to achieve a really thick batter. Season with salt and pepper. Leave to relax for about half an hour.

Heat the oil. It is hot enough when you drop a teaspoon of batter in and it immediately sizzles.

Dip the huss in the batter, try not to lose the ginger and gently lower into the oil. A slotted spoon is good for this. Cook for 4-5 minutes.

Don't put too many pieces in at once. Allow plenty of space round each piece.

Drain on kitchen paper.

Serve with a small bowl of soy sauce and a dish of lemon wedges.

~   ~   ~

JOHN DORY

John Dory	*Zeus faber*
Guernsey French	*Jean doraï* (m)
Jersey French	*Jean doré* (m), *dorée* (f)
French	*St Pierre*

This is really a Mediterranean species which does find its way further north. It is a very unusual, thin, fish. It can't swim very fast either, so stealth is the name of its game. It stalks its victim which can't see the predator that well because of it thinness. Suddenly, large jaws grab the unfortunate prey.

They tend to be more bone than flesh but the flesh that is there is very delicious. It is expensive because of the small amount of flesh but its delicate and distinctive flavour can command a high price. Market size is about 30-40 cm / 12-15 inches and it is available all year round.

It is easy to recognise because of its thinness and distinctive black spot or thumb mark behind the head. It has large tough spines and a smooth skin. The head is large and ugly. It is steely grey in colour but with a tinge of gold.

Some say that the distinctive black 'thumb print' behind the gills is that of St Peter – hence the French name. Then there is Dory to think about. Did Dory come from the French word *doreé* which means golden as the fish does have a golden sheen? The 'John' bit, I give up on!

The flesh is sought after for its sweetness and firmness. The head is important for fish soups. It is a difficult fish to fillet so let your fish-monger do that. The fish happily takes other flavours such as vermouth, white wine, orange, pernod and many herbs

John Dory with Fennel

Serves 4
4 fillets approx 150g/5oz each
1 fat bulb fennel
30g/1oz butter
1tsp caraway seeds

150ml/5 fl oz white wine
150ml/5 fl oz cream
1 tbsp Pernod (or similar)
2 tbsp olive oil
Salt and pepper

Finely shred the fennel. Fry it in 2 tbsp olive oil. Season and sprinkle with caraway seeds. When soft transfer to a buttered ovenproof dish.

Lay the fillets on top. Season and add the white wine. Cover with foil and cook in a hot oven for 10/15 minutes.

Remove the foil and drain as much of the juice as possible into the pan you cooked the fennel in. Add the cream and Pernod and whisk until reduced and creamy. Pour over the fillets.

Serve with skinned, chopped and fried tomatoes, topped with scissored chives and a bowl of buttered new potatoes.

John Dory with Mushrooms

Serves 4	150ml/5oz cream
4 fillets of 150g/5oz each	1 lemon
500g/1lb button mushrooms	Chopped parsley for garnishing
2/3 rashers streaky bacon	60g/2 oz butter + extra for frying fillets
1 medium onion or 2/3 shallots	Salt and pepper
150ml/5 fl oz white wine	Flour for coating

Chop the shallots or onion and gently fry in the butter until transparent. Take out and keep to one side. In the same pan, fry the chopped streaky bacon. Add the finely sliced mushrooms and cook for a further 3 to 4 minutes. Add the cooked shallots or onion. Transfer to a dish and keep warm.

Fry the floured fillets in butter until golden brown. Remove with a fish slice or spatula to a plate. Cover and keep warm.

Add the wine to the pan, bring to the boil, add the lemon juice, season and reduce until thickish. Remove from the heat and add the cream.

Place a fillet on each plate with a mound of onion, mushroom and bacon mixture alongside. Gently pour the sauce over the fish and around the mound. Sprinkle with chopped parsley.

Serve with boiled rice which has had a knob of butter added and a handful of chopped herbs.

MACKEREL

Atlantic Mackerel	*Scomber scombrus*
Guernsey French	*macré, macro, des makériaouts* or *macrillots*(m)
Jersey French	*maqu'sé* (m)
French	*maquereau bleu* (m)

Mackerel must have been a prime catch around the Channel Islands since time immemorial. The salting and export of mackerel was a significant trade from the Middle Ages until the 16th Century. Salted mackerel, together with salted conger, was exported as far as Gascony and it wasn't until the arrival of cheaper salted cod from Newfoundland that this local industry waned.

Folklore has it that if the gorse flower was prolific in Spring then there would be a good mackerel season. The term 'mackerel sky', signifying good weather, was an early form of meteorology dating from those days.

Mackereling was a way of life and fishermen's wives went around the parishes calling "macro, macro", selling their husband's catches.

Sadly, the 'penny' mackerel is a thing of the past....

The word in French – *maquereau* – means 'pimp', 'dandy' or 'flashy' and certainly the mackerel is flashy.

Mackerel is an oily fish therefore very beneficial healthwise.

The mackerel is a beautiful, elongated smooth fish with an iridescent blue-green back paling to silver sides and belly. It has a deep forked tail.

It grows up to about 45 cms. The flesh is an agreeable buff colour. An autumn caught mackerel is much paler in colour as by then there is less oil in the flesh.

They swim in shoals in the open upper waters of the sea from spring to autumn when they retire to deeper waters staying on the seabed, almost hibernating, and not eating. A winter-caught mackerel is a disappointment because it hasn't been feeding.

Mackerel do not keep well and need to be gutted straight away. Outside is the best place for gutting as it tends to be a bit of a messy business.

Mackerel can be fried, baked, grilled or soused. They can be cooked whole, filleted or butterfly-boned.

They are wonderful, too, cooked whole on the barbecue.

Sauces such as gooseberry, lemon and rhubarb go well with mackerel.

My favourite way of cooking mackerel is to toss in flour, fry in half oil/butter until golden brown and serve with a wedge of lemon and plain boiled potatoes. What could be simpler!

Grilled Mackerel with Sorrel Sauce

Serves 4
4 medium sized mackerel.

Sauce

120g/ 4 oz wild or cultivated sorrel	150ml/ 5 fl oz cream
60g/ 2 oz butter	Seasoning

Sorrel is common in fields and hedgerows thoughout the islands. The elongated shield-shaped leaves start appearing in the early spring. That is when it is at its best but it can be picked from the stalks well into May and June.

Sorrel is also cultivated and can be bought bagged, in punnets or bunches.

Remember that sorrel needs very little cooking.

First of all prepare the fish by gutting. Make 3 or 4 slashes either side of the fish and grill 3-4 minutes on each side – it's as simple as that!

Melt the butter in a small pan and put to one side. Prepare the sorrel by removing the stalks. Place the leaves one on top of the other, roll up tightly, like a cigar, and slice thinly across. Add the sorrel to the butter and with a wooden spoon, stir gently until the sorrel collapses; it needs only a whisper of cooking. As soon as the sorrel has collapsed and turned a pale sage green it is ready for the cream and seasoning to be added. It is quite a chunky sauce but the slightly acidic flavour is something special.

Serve straight away with the grilled mackerel.

Fried Mackerel with Tomatoes and Onion

This is a very local recipe as both tomatoes and mackerel are generally plentiful when in season.

4 medium sized mackerel either filleted or butterfly boned
2 onions
30g/1 oz butter
1 kilo/ 2 lbs tomatoes
Spikes of rosemary, sage leaves or sprigs of thyme

Fry the onions in butter (in days gone by, it would be dripping) till transparent, add the chopped up tomatoes, season, add your chosen herb. Gently simmer till you have a mushy pureé.

Flour the fish. Fry gently in a mixture of oil and butter on both sides. Serve with boiled potatoes and the mushy tomatoes.

Another very local dish is **Mackerel with Mustard**.

Fillets of mackerel were coated in a mixture of dry mustard and flour and fried.

Another way is to mix the mustard with vinegar, then coat the flesh with it. Lightly flour the fillets and then fry them 2 minutes on each side.

Soused Mackerel

Serves 4

A useful thing to be able to do when there is a glut as soused mackerel can be kept for up to 1 week.

Fillet 4 fish and lay them in an ovenproof dish.

Finely slice an onion and put in a saucepan, add 1 small cup of granulated sugar, 1 small cup of malt vinegar and 1 small cup of water.

Add 5 or 6 cloves, 5 or 6 crushed cardamom pods, 6 black peppercorns, 1 tsp salt and 2 or 3 bay leaves. Bring all to the boil. Simmer for 10 to 15 minutes till the onion is transparent.

Pour over the mackerel. Cover with a lid or foil and bake gently in a preheated oven 180C/350F Gas 4 for 40 minutes.

Leave to cool then refrigerate.

Mackerel Escabèche

Escabèche is a preparation of fried fish which has been allowed to cool and is then soused with a hot marinate of vinegar and other ingredients.

Serves 4

4 fillets mackerel, 8 if they are small
1 lemon
Salt
Flour for coating
Oil such as sunflower for frying oil
Sauce
200ml/ 6 floz red wine vinegar
6 peppercorns
half tsp coriander seeds

half tsp cumin seeds
2 cloves
2 cloves garlic
Small piece of cinnamon stick
2 bay leaves
1 tsp sugar
90 ml/ 3 fl oz olive oil
1 red chilli
Salt and pepper

Lay the fillets in a dish. Sprinkle with salt and lemon juice.

Crush the peppercorns, coriander, cumin seeds and cloves. Add the garlic and blend to make a paste.

In a small saucepan, put the vinegar, bay leaves, cinnamon stick, sugar, seeded and sliced chilli, (leave the seeds in if you enjoy a hot taste). Bring to the boil. Add the crushed spices, garlic paste and olive oil. Simmer for 10 to 15 minutes. Keep hot.

Coat the fillets with flour and fry. Put back in the rinsed dish. Pour the sauce over and leave for about 2 hours, spooning some of the juice over every now and again.

Serve cold with plain boiled new potatoes.

Mackerel Paté

Serves 4
4 plump fillets of smoked mackerel
60g/ 2oz melted butter
2 tbsp plain yoghourt – alternatively use crème fraîche
1 tbsp horseradish sauce
1 lemon
Black pepper (salt isn't necessary)

Remove the skin and place the smoked mackerel in the food processor. Add the cooled melted butter, lemon juice, horseradish sauce and yoghourt. Season with black pepper.

Whizz until smooth, if too thick add a little more lemon juice but you don't want it sloppy otherwise you will have difficulty serving it.

Spoon into a small bowl or 4 ramekin dishes and chill for about 3 hours.

This can happily be made the day before and will last at least 4-5 days.

Serve with lots of crusty bread and mayonnaise or tartare sauce.

MONKFISH

Monkfish, Angler-fish	*Lophius piscatorius*
Guernsey French	*violon* (m), *ànge de mer* (f) or *rogne dé maïr* (f)
Jersey French	*mouaine* (m)
French	*lotte* (f), *baudroie* (f)

In France the white flesh has always been sought after because of its flavour and versatility. The opposite seemed to be the case in Britain, until recently, when at last it is being appreciated. The flesh is very versatile and can be likened to lobster or scampi for its texture. The head is excellent used in making fish soup.

Not the most handsome of fish – its name too is puzzling. It behaves in the opposite way to a monk. There is no charity as it waits, hardly breathing to snap up its prey using its great ugly jaws ready to devour whatever passes as it lies on the sea-bed. There is no honesty either as it is a master of deception, its mottled skin creating an excellent camouflage; also the 'antenna' on the top of its head is used to lure unwary prey.

At the fish-mongers, the monkfish is usually displayed without its head, which might otherwise put off potential buyers!

I was talking to a friend who contradicted all that I said about the ugliness of the monkfish. He thinks it is beautiful and well adapted for its life-style! As the old saying goes: 'beauty is in the eye of the beholder'.

When buying monkfish, choose from a biggish fish, often the smaller tails are disappointing.

Monkfish goes well with strong flavours such as anchovy, bacon and ginger.

Monkfish Roasted with Parma Ham and Anchovies

Serves 4
Piece of skinned monkfish approx 1 kilo/ 2 lbs
50g (2oz) tin flat anchovies - drained
4 slices parma ham 1 tbsp lemon juice + 4 wedges for serving
750g/1½ lbs potatoes

2 onions	60ml/ 2 fl oz olive oil
6 cloves garlic	250g/8oz courgettes
2 sprigs rosemary	Salt and pepper

With a sharp knife, ease the two fillets away from the bone. Cut these in two as you need 4 similar sized pieces.

Finely chop or pound the drained anchovy fillets – use only half the tin of anchovies, if you don't like too strong a flavour. Add the lemon juice and spread the paste over the monkfish. Wrap the parma ham around each piece of fish as tightly as possible with the join underneath. If necessary, secure with tooth-picks.

Put to one side.

Into a roasting or ovenproof dish, finely slice the peeled potatoes, onions and garlic and scatter with scissored rosemary, season with salt and pepper. Pour over the olive oil.

Roast at 230C/450F Gas 8 for 20 minutes turning occasionally.

Remove from the oven. Add the fish so that it nestles amongst the potatoes and onions. Scald the finely sliced courgettes in boiling salted water, drain and scatter around the fish, drizzle a little oil over.

Roast for 25 minutes in a hot oven. Test to make sure the monkfish pieces are cooked. Don't forget about the tooth-picks.

Rest for 5 minutes and serve.

Monkfish with Tomato & Ginger

Serves 4

750g/1½lbs skinned monkfish
Flour for coating
Sauce
1kilo/2lbs tomatoes
2 medium onions
2 cloves garlic
Piece of fresh ginger, approx 5 cms/2in long
1 tsp cumin

Juice of 1 lemon
150ml/5 fl oz dry white wine
1 level tsp sugar
2 tbsp olive oil
Salt and pepper
Wedges of lemon to accompany

Make the sauce first.

Slice and fry the onions in olive oil until transparent. Add the garlic and cook for a further minute.

Peel and finely chop or grate the ginger and add to the onion along with the cumin. Season with salt and pepper. Add the roughly chopped tomatoes and 1 level tsp sugar. Add the lemon juice, white wine and a little water. Allow to bubble, then gently simmer until cooked and thickened.

Sieve into a small saucepan. Cover.

Cut the monkfish into cubes and flour. Heat the olive oil in a pan. When hot, add the monkfish and fry until golden brown on all sides, about 6 to 8 minutes.

Place a dollop of the tomato and ginger mixture on each plate. Pile the monkfish cubes on top.

Serve with the lemon wedges and perhaps buttered noodles to which you have added any finely chopped herbs you may have at hand.

Monkfish with Prawn Sauce

Serve 4

750g/1½ lbs monkfish skinned and in one piece if possible with the backbone removed

550ml/ 20 fl oz court bouillon

Make the court bouillon with 400ml/14 fl oz water, 150ml/5 fl oz dry white wine, 1 chopped carrot, 1 sliced stalk celery, 2 bay leaves, seasoning.

Gently bring all the above ingredients to the boil. Simmer for 20 to 30 minutes. Strain and reduce by half.

Sauce:

250g/8oz shelled cooked prawns + 8 extra to go with the fish

30g/1 oz flour	1 tbsp chopped chives
30g/1 oz butter	1 tbsp chopped parsley
150 ml/ 5 fl oz cream	Salt and pepper

Wash and trim the monkfish, place in a wide-based saucepan so that it can all fit in and lie flat. Strain the court bouillon over the fish.

Cover, bring gently to the boil and simmer for approx. 15 minutes, until it is cooked.

Lift the monkfish out and place on a serving dish. Cover with foil and keep warm. Reserve the court bouillon

In a saucepan, melt the butter, add the flour and mix well. Add as much as you need of the reserved court bouillon, gently stirring all the time until the sauce is smooth.

Add the prawns to the sauce along with the chopped chives and parsley. Season with salt and pepper.

Remove from the heat. Add the cream.

Arrange the remaining whole prawns around the fish. Pour some of the sauce over the fish, serving the remainder separately.

Hollandaise sauce can be used as an alternative to the prawn sauce.

Alternatively, the fish can be allowed to go cold. Serve with mayonnaise but add some chopped parsley and chives.

PILCHARD

Pilchard	*Sardina pilchardus*
Guernsey French	*sardaenne* (f)
Jersey French	*sardinne* (f)
French	*sardine* (f)

Sardines are dealt with later but they are young pilchards. The reason pilchards are more common on the fishmonger's slab is because they venture into our colder waters leaving the younger ones behind in the warmer waters off Portugal.

A stream-lined silvery blue fish with distinctive scales which have to be removed before cooking. Gutting is necessary but the fish is usually cooked whole.

There seems to be some sort of 'hang-up' over pilchards and sardines. If offered the choice, probably the sardine would be chosen and yet it is the same fish. Is it the memory of tinned pilchards in tomato sauce that turns us off?

Both lend themselves to barbecueing, their silvery skin becoming crisply baked. With the aid of hinged barbecue grills, that tendency to stick to whatever they were cooked on has gone, or at least been reduced!

Grilled Pilchards

Serves 4
4 pilchards – depending on size
Brush the pilchards with a little oil
Grill the gutted pilchards quickly about 2 minutes on each side.
Serve with lots of lemon wedges.
Alternatively, they could be barbecued.

Baked Pilchards

Pilchards cook very well in the oven..

Lay the cleaned pilchards on an oiled baking tray, drizzle with lemon juice, sprinkle with chopped herbs of your choice, season and bake in a hot oven for 10-15 minutes until browned and sizzling.

Serve with a green salad, crusty bread and perhaps a bowl of hommus or babaganoush – recipes at end.

Mustard Baked Pilchards

Serves 4
4 plump pilchards
30g/1oz butter
1tbsp dry mustard
Salt and pepper

Mash the butter with the mustard, salt and pepper then melt it.

Brush on both sides of the gutted pilchards.

Lay on an oiled baking tray and bake in a hot oven for 10-15 minutes.

Serve with a green salad and new potatoes that have been tossed in melted butter along with 1tbsp chopped parsley.

PLAICE

Plaice	*Pleuronectes platessa*
Guernsey french	*plaïe* (f)
Jersey french	*pliaie* (f)
French	*plie* (f) or *carrelet* (m)

Distinctive flatfish, easily recognised by its colouring. The slightly humped upper side is brown with red or orange spots. The underside is white. It is a right-eyed flatfish which means that both eyes are on the right side of the body. Plaice lie on the seabed, partly covering themselves with sand so they are really well disguised. They grow up to about 40 cms/16inches. They feed on small crustaceans, molluscs and worms.

Plaice are available all year round but are best from May to December.

Plaice can be cooked whole or filleted.

When cooking on the bone, remove the head along with the gut. With a knife or a pair of scissors cut away the fins. Rinse and pat dry.

There are many ways of serving plaice, grilled, fried, rolled or baked. It is a very delicate fish needing very little cooking.

As plaice fillets are generally small, you will need two per person, unless of course you find a whopper! The fillets from the dark upper side are much plumper than those from the underside.

Serving a whole fish, you will need one per person.

Grilled Plaice

With melted butter, brush the upper sides of the fillets or the whole fish. Season and place under a hot grill for 3/4 minutes. Turn, brush with butter and grill the other side. Serve with a wedge of lemon.

Fried Plaice

Flour the fillets with seasoned flour. Fry in butter for 5 minutes each side. The butter will give a crispiness and adds to the flavour. Serve with wedges of lemon.

New potatoes tossed in butter and 1tbsp chopped mint and parsley go deliciously well with grilled plaice.

Rolled Plaice Fillets with Tarragon and Shrimp Sauce

Serves 4

8 plaice fillets, each portion approx. 180g /6oz

1 small onion

1 tbsp tarragon vinegar

150ml/5fl oz dry white wine

1 tbsp chopped tarragon

1 tbsp chopped parsley

Shrimp sauce

120g/4oz cooked prawns or shrimp

150ml/5 fl oz cream

2 egg yolks

60g/2 oz butter

Salt and paprika

Season the fillets and loosely roll them so that the flesh is on the outside ending with the tail underneath. Place the rolled fillets in a flat casserole that will snugly hold them all. In this way, they will keep their shape and won't unroll.

In a frying pan or saucepan, fry the finely chopped onion in butter. Add the white wine, vinegar, chopped tarragon and seasoning.

Pour the mixture around the rolled fillets. Dot each fillet with butter. Cover with foil and cook in a hot oven for 8-10 minutes.

Carefully lift the rolled fillets onto a warm serving dish.

Strain the liquid into a small saucepan. Whisk in the egg yolks to thicken it. Bring almost to the boil then add the chopped prawns or shrimps and a good pinch of paprika.

Gently heat again. Finally add the cream but don't boil. Pour over the fish, sprinkle with the chopped parsley.

Serve with buttered and parsleyed new potatoes and florets of broccoli.

~   ~   ~

Red Mullet

Striped Red Mullet	*Mullus surmuletus*
Guernsey french	*rouage mulet* (m) or *rouge molet* (m)
Jersey french	*mulet rouage* (m)
French	*rouget de roche* (m)

This is a most attractive small fish growing up to 40 cms / 16 inches. One tends to get drawn towards red mullet because of its beautiful iridescence. It is covered in large reddish scales which pale to yellow on the sides and gold on the belly. It has a blunt snout with two barbels under the chin.

It is available during the winter months from October to March.

As with the grey mullet, it is caught by anglers and in gill nets.

It is an ideal fish for grilling or baking in the oven.

Filleting is fiddly and is best done by your fishmonger.

Small fish are good additions to fish soup.

Red mullet have a very distinct flavour, almost crabby, because of their diet. They are found mainly on sandy and rocky sea-beds.

Barbecued or Grilled Red Mullet

Serves 4

4 mullet each weighing 250g/8oz (alternatively use rainbow trout or bass)
120g/4oz rocket (watercress is a good alternative)

2 shallots	Seasoning
1 large clove garlic	60g/2oz butter

Scale and gut the mullet, taking care to keep the liver. Rinse and dry, season the cavity. Slash the fish 2 or 3 times on both sides.

Chop the shallots and garlic very finely and mix with the chopped rocket. Place a little of the rocket mixture along with the chopped liver in the cavity. Dot with a little butter in the slashes.

Place any remaining rocket in the grill pan. Lie the mullet on top, (closely together so that the mixture doesn't fall out). Under a hot grill, cook for 3-4 minutes on both sides.

If you are concerned about the stuffing falling out, then tie string around each mullet, removing it at the end of cooking.

Barbecuing: Having filled the mullet with stuffing and tied them, place them in a hinged wire fish rack and cook till blistery and browned, approx 5 minutes on both sides.

Remove the string.

Serve with perhaps a mixed green salad with lots of rocket. Alternatively, a tomato salad with a little crumbled feta cheese, black olives and torn basil leaves and dressed with lemon juice and olive oil, salt and plenty black pepper. A bowl of minted new potatoes to compliment the al fresco meal.

Red Mullet with Red & Green Peppers

Serves 4
4 red mullet each approx. 250g/8oz, if small, use 2 per person
1 red and 1 green pepper

1 small onion	1 tsp ground coriander
1 clove garlic	1 tsp chopped fresh ginger
Juice of 1 lemon	Salt and pepper
1 tsp ground cumin	3 tbsp olive oil

Prepare the mullet by scaling and emptying the cavity. Make 2-3 diagonal slashes on both sides. Lay in an oiled oven-proof dish. Season and drizzle with oil.

Cook in a preheated oven 220C/425F Gas 7 for 15-20 minutes.

Grilling or barbecuing is an alternative way of cooking.

While cooking, fry the chopped onion and garlic in the remaining oil until transparent. Add the finely sliced peppers turning till well coated and beginning to collapse, adding a little more oil if necessary. Add the cumin, coriander and ginger, season with salt and pepper. Remove from the heat, add the lemon juice and keep warm.

Serve each mullet on a plate along with some pepper mixture arranged alongside.

Red Mullet with Forcemeat Cakes and Mushrooms

Serves 4
4 fillets of a good 180g/6oz each or 8 fillets to make up approx the same weight
Try and choose your fish so that you can have the livers

250g/8oz mushrooms	1 tbsp chopped parsley
90g/3oz breadcrumbs	60g/2oz butter
2 shallots	Oil for frying
Grated rind of 1 lemon	Salt and pepper
1 egg yolk	

Start by making the forcemeat cakes.

In a basin mix the breadcrumbs, finely chopped shallots, grated lemon, salt and pepper and chopped parsley. Chop the livers and add. Bind with the egg yolk and a little lemon juice, if necessary. Divide the mixture into 8 small balls, flattening to make small cakes.

Fry gently until golden on both sides. Keep warm.

Slice the mushrooms and gently fry in butter till the juices run. Keep warm.

Coat the mullet with seasoned flour and fry in the same pan with a little extra olive oil. Two minutes on each side is long enough.

Serve on 4 plates along with the mushrooms and forcemeat cakes and wedges of lemon.

~   ~   ~

ROCKLING

Five bearded rockling	*Ciliata mustela*
Three bearded and largest rockling	*Gaidropsarus vulgaris*
Guernsey French	*louche* or *p'tite louache* (f), *lochu* (m), *loche* (m) and *alputte* (f)
Jersey French	*vra* (m)
French	*Loup* (m)

Rockling or Rocky as it is known locally is a small fish found around the coast. It lives in rock pools and along the rocky shore. As a result of its diet of shrimps and other small crustaceans, it has firm tasty flesh with a certain crabbiness about it, similar to red mullet.

It grows to about 20 cms. It is a reddish brown with 4 barbels on the upper lip and one on the chin. It has long dorsal and anal fins.

It is not a 'commercial' fish. It tends to be caught by shore fishermen who take them to the market but they are never in great numbers.

The larger, three-bearded rockling is caught in pots and sometimes sold at retail.

As a child I remember that it was the first fish I ever caught and that was just luck. We were spending the day at Grandes Rocques and, having enjoyed lots of swimming, we decided to have a go at fishing. My fish was about 10cms long but to me it was the biggest fish in the sea! I don't think my Mother could be bothered to dirty a pan for such small fry so we gave it to the cat and because it was raw, puss wouldn't eat it!

But if you have one big enough, it is worth filleting and frying.

Just cut off the head, gut, toss in flour, fry in a mixture of oil and butter and serve with lemon wedges.

It is an ideal addition to fish soups.

SALMON

Salmon	*Salmo salar*
Seatrout	*salmo trutta*
Guernsey French	*saumoan* (m)
Jersey French	*saumon* (m)
	Brown trout – *eune truite*
French	*saumon* (m) and *truite de mer* (f)

I was going to start by saying that salmon are not caught in these waters but I am assured that occasionally they are as they make their way towards French rivers.

Although not usually a 'local' fish, salmon is so delicious, readily available and easy to use that I felt I must include several recipes.

Price-wise, farmed salmon compares very favourably with other fish whereas, in the past, it was considered a luxury. Having said that, wild salmon is of course expensive.

Salmon is easily recognisable as it is a large fish, growing up to 80-100cm / 32-40 inches, with a silvery blue back with scattered black markings, silvery sides and belly. Its small scales are easily rubbed off.

Seatrout (which is a brown trout that has gone to sea) is similar in appearance, but is smaller.

Wild salmon is superior in flavour and colour. (Recently, I read somewhere that wild versus farmed salmon can be compared with wild boar and pork chops!)

It is at its best from February to August.

Farmed salmon is available all year round. It is excellent in taste and texture but does not have the richness and colour of the wild. Richard Lord tells me that 1,000,000 tons of farmed salmon are produced every year.

I did ask Jerry Cobb, who was one of our former local fishmongers, how you can tell a wild from a farmed one. His reply was that a farmed one has a blunt snout from always being up against the netting at the end of the pens. I don't know if he was pulling my leg or not!

With the advent of farmed salmon, it has become almost an everyday meal but having said that it is still something delicious. For a special occasion, a whole salmon does give a sense of drama – as well as looking spectacular it tastes good, and another plus is that it is easily cooked and dressed.

How do I cook a whole salmon?

There are various ways of cooking a salmon whole. I prefer simply wrapping the fish in foil. The salmon is wrapped like a parcel thus retaining all the juices.

If the salmon is to be served cold, coax into a crescent-shape and perhaps use a smaller roasting tin. If serving hot, than a straighter shape is better.

Served hot or cold, salmon is always a winner. So don't be put off by thinking you haven't the right vessel to cook it in or a roasting pan big enough. You will surely find something suitable in your cupboard or can borrow from a neighbour.

And once the party is over save all the remaining bits clinging to the body to make fish-cakes, a mousse or coulibiac.

So, hopefully having persuaded you that you can cook a whole one, let us start.

Whole Salmon Cooked in Foil

Serves 6
1 whole small salmon weighing approximately $2\frac{1}{2}$ kilo/ 5 lbs
Serves 10
1 whole salmon weighing approximately 4 kilos/8lbs
To serve 20
1 whole salmon weighing approximately 7 kilos to 14 lbs

Rub the salmon with salt, this will remove excess scales. Rinse under running water. Don't bother to dry it as the water helps to steam it.

Take a generous piece of extra strong foil. Lay the salmon diagonally across the foil. Season it with salt and pepper, a scattering of any herbs you might have at hand such as thyme or bay leaf, the juice of a lemon squeezed along its length. Wrap the fish firmly into a parcel, ensuring that the join is along the top of the fish.

Before placing in the tin, take two pieces, about 3cms/ 2 inches wide of doubled foil or muslin or similar material. Place them across the roasting tin. Now place the salmon on top – this will help to lift it out of the tin at the end of its cooking time.

Add water so that it comes to about half-way up the tin but not covering the parceled fish. The parcel must not stick or the foil may tear when you lift it out and the juice lost.

Cook in a preheated oven 190C/375F, Gas 5.

A fish weighing 3 kilos/ 6 lbs would take 1 hour.

For a fish bigger than 3 kilos/6 lbs, reduce the heat half way through the cooking time so that the water is barely moving.

The aim is to cook it slowly and gently. When the cooking time is up, make sure the fish is cooked by tearing the foil near the head as this is the thickest part of the body. Insert a sharp pointed knife, easing it into the flesh at an angle so that you can gently lift the flesh away from the bone. If it still clings then cook a little longer till the flesh comes away from the bone and the skin peels off easily.

To Serve Cold

When cold, lift out the salmon carefully and place on its serving dish, leaving the foil on, to retain the natural moistness.

Shortly before serving, neatly roll back the foil and remove the upper skin which is thick enough to almost peel off. Don't try to remove the foil under the fish.

A cold whole samon is often the star of a buffet table and thus merits attractive presentation. Surround it with fresh herbs – parsley for example – or flowers, such as nasturtiums or marigolds or a combination of these.

Serve with mayonnaise or sauce tartare.

To Serve Hot

When beginning to cool a little, lift out the salmon carefully and place on its serving dish.

Carefully roll back (but don't remove) the foil, to expose the fish.

Several carefully placed bay leaves or sprigs of parsley will dignify this naturally beautiful fish.

Peel back the skin before serving.

Accompany with a béchamel, hollandaise or white sauce to which has been added finely grated lemon peel and chopped parsley.

Salmon Cutlets or Steaks

These can be cooked by grilling, poaching or frying. Barbecued either in foil, in a hinged wire rack or grill.

Depending on the thickness of the steaks, cooking would take about 3 or 4 minutes on each side. If wrapped in foil, cooking would take a little longer.

For frying, a heavy duty ridged frying pan is good, especially non-stick. Whether frying or grilling, allow 3 to 4 minutes on each side.

Poaching can be either on top or in the oven. Poach in water for approximately 8 to 10 minutes.

Salmon Mousse

Serves 6 as a starter or 4 as a main course

This can be made from the leftovers from a whole salmon. If starting from scratch, the tail ends of salmon and other cheaper pieces are ideal. A small amount of smoked salmon will enhance the flavour. Use either one large mould or individual ramekins.

500g/1 lb cooked or uncooked salmon

60g/ 2 oz smoked salmon	150ml / 5 fl oz double cream
Scant 15g / half oz gelatine	Juice of 1 lemon
3 egg whites	Seasoning

If using uncooked fish, poach in 275ml/ 10 fl oz using water or half water and white wine for 10-15 minutes. Drain off the liquid into a bowl and leave the fish to cool.

Measure 5 tbsp of the cooking liquor into a bowl and sprinkle the gelatine on top. Gently whisk it in and leave to dissolve. The bowl can be placed in a saucepan or larger bowl of hot water to help the gelatine to dissolve but do not rush it or the gelatine will stubbornly refuse to dissolve.

Remove any bones and skin. Place the fish in a blender or food processor along with the smoked salmon. Add the melted gelatine and the lemon juice and give a quick whizz.

Empty into a mixing bowl.

Whisk the cream till thick but not firm. Fold into the fish mixture.

In another bowl whisk the egg whites to soft peaks. Add to the salmon and cream mixture. Season and spoon into a lightly oiled mould or oiled ramekins, using a bland oil such as sunflower.

If you are nervous about turning them out, line the ramekins or mould with cling film.

Refrigerate for at least 3 hours.

Once turned out, decorate with a scissoring of chives or fennel and serve surrounded by something green such as water-cress or fronds of dill.

Salmon Fish Cakes

Once again, these can be made from cooked or uncooked salmon. This is a satisfying dish, especially served with a parsley sauce that is more green than white. A green vegetable such as calibrese, courgettes or peas is all that is needed to go with the fish cakes.

Serves 4
375g/12 oz fish
250g/8oz mashed potato (don't add any milk or butter)
2 eggs   30g/1 oz butter
1 tbsp chopped parsley   1 tbsp oil
Fresh breadcrumbs   Salt and pepper

If using uncooked fish, poach in a little water but cover to help cook the top. Drain, reserving the liquor for the sauce.

In a bowl flake the fish and add the mashed potato, egg yolks, parsley and season with salt and pepper. Gently mix together with a fork till all binds.

Using your hands shape into 8 cakes. I try to avoid too perfect a shape as taking the trouble to make them means you don't want something resembling readymade.

Whisk the egg whites in a bowl, coat each cake with breadcrumbs and leave to rest in the fridge for at least an hour.

Heat the oil and butter and fry gently for 5 minutes until you have a crisp underside, turn and cook the other side.

Serve with wedges of lemon and a really green parsley sauce, made with the reserved liquor or with milk.

SARDINE

Sardine	*Sardina pilchardus*
Guernsey French	*sardaenne* (f)
Jersey French	*sardinne* (f)
French	*sardine*

Sardines are young pilchards. They are left behind when the bigger pilchards migrate to the colder northern waters, preferring the warmer waters off Portugal and the Meditteranean to grow in.

A small silvery fish with a dark blue back, silvery sides and belly, seldom growing more than 15 cms. They swim in great shoals and tend to get 'hoovered up'. Stocks were becoming so depleted that strict controls had to be introduced.

Until the early 1950s most of us knew sardines as something that came out of a tin. Travelling as we do, many of us have come to enjoy them in their natural state (not in a tin!). They are available fresh and frozen.

Here is a recipe from our Cook, Fidèla, who used to cook them regularly for us in Casablanca. She served the dish with a green salad made with endive, the frizzy mophead salad, sprinkled with sea salt, ground black pepper, olive oil and lemon juice. The bitterness of the endive balanced the richness of the sardines.

Fidela's Recipe

Serves 4
1 kilo/ 2lbs sardines
1 tbsp ground cumin

1 tbsp ground coriander
Salt and pepper
Juice of 2 lemons

Cut off the heads, dragging the innards with them, wash carefully. Arrange in an earthenware casserole so that they fit tightly. Sprinkle with the cumin, coriander and lemon juice, season and add just enough water to cover the bottom to prevent them sticking.

Place in a moderate oven 180C/350F Gas 4 for an hour. Check that there is liquid, reduce the heat to 140C/275F Gas 1 and cook for another hour.

Leave them to cool before serving with the salad. A dish of lemon wedges to help cut the richness.

Baked Sardines

Prepare the same quantities as for the above recipe. Lay them on an oiled baking tray, sprinkle with chopped herbs of your choice, drizzle with lemon juice, season and bake in a hot oven for 10/15 minutes.

Alternatively they can be prepared as for the recipe above. Either grill or fry them. If barbecueing, use a hinged rack, being small they are difficult to handle.

Skate

Skate, Ray	*Raja brachyura* – blonde ray
	Raja clavata – thornback ray
Guernsey French	*d'la raie* (f) – blonde or mottled
	grison (m) – grey ray
Jersey French	*raie* (f) or *cârée* (f)
French	*raie* (f)
	raie bouclée (f) – thornback ray

Ray and skate refer to the same species. The Common ray used to be familiar in local waters but is now almost extinct.

There are two main types, the Thornback Ray or Roker and the Blonde Ray.

The thornback ray is fished a lot off Jersey while the blonde ray is fished off the Casquets near Alderney and the Schole bank – 'the banks'.

Also seen in our markets are the undulate and small-eyed ray. The undulate is more common.

Ray/Skate is available all year round but is best in winter.

They have large diamond shaped bodies with a long thin tail. The back is olivy green or brown with dark and light spots, while underneath is creamy white.

They live and feed on the bottom but will come to the surface to catch other fish. Like the dogfish, the female lays her eggs in horny cases known as a 'mermaid's purses' which hook themselves to rocky surfaces till the baby is ready to hatch.

In the past one would find these little black purses washed up on the beach but not so much now.

Skate is a cartilaginous fish with pinkish flesh. The pectoral fins or wings are eaten. Skate or ray 'knobs' are also very good. They come from the head and are the cheek mouth muscles.

It is important not to eat skate straight from the sea. It must be allowed to relax and develop its flavour. Herbert Nichols tells me that when he caught a skate he would wait until the next day to sell it.

It is possible that skate/ray develops a slight smell of ammonia. To counteract this, dip the ray in milk or sqeeze lemon juice all over. Thorough washing also helps. As the fish cooks, the smell disappears.

I was surprised to hear that skate was used by 'fish and chip' shops. It would be battered and fried and served with chips and was very popular too. In fact skate is a great favourite with locals.

I must just tell you of an experience I had in Tripoli, Libya, where my boyfriend (now my husband) was working with an overseas bank. I donned a pair of flippers and goggles and off we went. Suddenly underneath me, I saw about six huge things that looked rather like army blankets flapping their way gracefully beneath me. They turned out to be giant sting rays, a cousin of our skate.

I had never seen anything like that in my life and swam to the shore as fast as I could. My boyfriend said I went off so fast I seemed to be running on the surface!

I remembered stories of the sting in their tails which, of course, they never use unless very disturbed.

Off the Cayman Islands, people swim amongst rays and even stroke them!

Baked Skate with Caper Sauce

Serves 4

4 wing pieces preferably from towards the centre of the body as they are thicker and meatier. Each piece weighing about 250g/8oz

2 tbsp capers	Ground black pepper and salt
60g/2 oz butter	Juice of 1 lemon
150 ml/5 fl oz white wine	1 tbsp chopped parsley

Butter the ovenproof dish or roasting tin. Place therein the wing pieces of skate. Divide the butter into 4 and place a quarter on each wing. Scatter the capers over. Grind with black pepper, season with salt and add the lemon juice and wine.

Cover with foil and put in a hot oven 200C/400F Gas 6 for 10 minutes. Remove the foil and allow to cook for a further 20mins. Make sure it is cooked by taking a knife and easing a piece of meat from the bone. If it comes away easily, it is done. Don't overcook, otherwise it will become dry.

Place on a serving dish and pour the buttery juice over each piece. Scatter with chopped parsley.

Skate Mayonnaise

Serves 4

Skate is excellent cold. It can be served on the wing but it is perhaps more enjoyable if the meat is removed and rearranged in a 'fish shape'.

4 skate wings approx. 250g/8oz each

Juice of 1 lemon	275ml/10 fl oz mayonnaise
30g/1oz butter	1 tbsp chopped parsley
Salt	1 tbsp chopped chives
Black pepper	1 tbsp chopped black olives

Place the skate wings in a roasting tin. Divide the butter into 4 and put a quarter on each. Season and sprinkle with lemon juice. Add 150ml/5 fl oz water (just to prevent sticking), cover with foil and place in a pre-heated oven 200C/400F Gas 6 for 30 minutes. Half way through cooking, baste with the juices. Alternatively, the skate can be poached.

At the end of the cooking time, check to make sure it is cooked by easing some of the flesh away from the cartilaginous bone.

While it is cooking, make the mayonnaise, see recipe on page 211.

Add most of the chopped parsley, chives and olives to the mayonnaise.

Once the skate is cooked, remove from the pan and allow to cool.

Remove the meat from the skate, take care not to break the ribs of flesh.

Arrange into a fish shape but, as you do so, add a little mayonnaise to bind it together. When you have a reasonable shape, coat with mayonnaise.

Decorate with herbs or flowers. Scissor a few chives on top.

Serve the remainder of the mayonnaise separately.

A green salad, preferably one of those frizzy endive ones which have a very slightly bitter taste is an excellent accompaniment.

A bowl of small potatoes washed and boiled in their skins and sprinkled with chopped parsley and a knob of butter would also go well.

SOLE

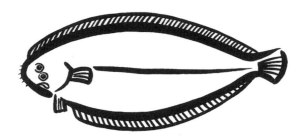

Dover sole	*Solea solea*
Lemon sole	*microstomus kitt*
There is also the sand sole	
Guernsey French	*sole* (m)
Jersey French	*sole* (m)
French	*sole acommune* (dover sole) and *limande sole* (lemon sole)

Dover sole

An elongated flatfish whose upper side is a mottled brown. It has a dark spot on the pectoral fin (behind the gill). The underside is white. It has a very slightly lopsided look about it as the eyes aren't evenly placed but slightly low down with its mouth to the right of them.

Dover sole grows up to 60 cms / 24 inches long and is available all year round but is best from March to December. Avoid a Dover sole that has recently spawned and looks thin and flaccid. Look for a thick, plump fish.

Years ago when I was doing an exchange with a French family, we were staying in their holiday home on the Chausey Islands. Most days at low tide, Monsieur Fortin would go to one of the sandy beaches. In the shallow water, about knee-deep, he would walk up and down holding in each hand, a sort of trident. Up and down the beach he went, with his trident's prongs sinking into the sand. Sure enough, he would very often spike a sole.

Lemon Sole

Lemon sole is related to plaice. It is broader than Dover sole. It is a sandy brown colour with a white underside. It is smaller too, up to about 40cm.

It is available all year round but is best from March to December. It is cheaper than Dover sole and can be cooked whole or as fillets. It is more popular than plaice because it is plumper.

Sole is a fish that freezes well.

Sole is popular because, once cooked, it comes off the bone very easily.

A whole grilled Dover, Lemon or sand sole are all firm favourites.

As children we were told, when eating a whole sole, never to turn it over on our plate to get to the meat underneath. This would mean that a boat out at sea would capsize!

Lift the backbone out and leave it to one side. This applies to all fish.

The following recipes apply to both Dover and Lemon sole.

Sole with Hollandaise Sauce

Serves 4

4 plump fillets	Stick of celery
Court Bouillon	6 crushed peppercorns
550ml/20 fl oz water	3 bay leaves
1 carrot	Juice of half a lemon
1 onion	Salt and pepper

The recipe for Hollandaise sauce given on page 210.

For the Court Bouillon, pour the water in the pan. Add the chopped carrot, onion and stick of celery, 6 crushed peppercorns, 3 bay leaves and juice of half a lemon. Simmer gently for about 30 minutes. You need to reduce the quantity by half.

Roll the fillets, skin side inside or keep them flat.

Place in a buttered shallow oven-proof casserole. Pour over the strained court bouillon. Cover and poach for 15 minutes at 180C/ 350F Gas 5.

While cooking, make the Hollandaise.

On serving, place the rolled fillets on individual plates. Pour a little sauce over and around each portion, scissor with chives.

Serve with new potatoes, including a green vegetable or salad to give colour.

Sole Normande

This is a more extravagant dish. Rich with butter, eggs and cream and of course mussels or oysters and button mushrooms. This is a sensational recipe.
It can be prepared well in advance. As you start your first course, just pop the sole into the oven. The sauce has to be finished but you will have done the basics.
The mushrooms can be left in a frying pan and reheated. The cooked mussels or oysters can also be ready and waiting for that final flourish.

Serves 4

4 plump sole fillets	Velouté Sauce
12/16 button mushrooms	60g/2oz butter
24 mussels or 8 oysters	60g/2oz pl. flour
150 ml /5 fl oz white wine	550ml/20fl oz (1pint) fish stock
90g/3oz butter	150 ml/5fl oz cream
1 tbsp lemon juice	Salt and pepper
3 egg yolks	Mushroom stalks
Salt and pepper	

Start by making the velouté sauce as it takes a long time (about 45 minutes). It has to reduce by half.

Melt the butter in a saucepan, add the flour stirring until smooth. Gradually add the fish stock, stirring or whisking again until smooth. Add the chopped mushroom stalks and bring gently to the boil. Place the saucepan into another that holds simmering water. If you have a double saucepan especially for sauces then so much the better. Allow the sauce to simmer gently so that it reduces to half, stir occasionally to prevent a skin forming. Strain, cover and keep warm.

Now cook the mussels. Pour the white wine into a large saucepan. No water is necessary as there is plenty of liquid in the mussels.

Add the mussels and cover the pan with a tight fitting lid. Cook, while shaking the pan for 2 minutes. Strain, and reserve the juice. Shell the mussels and discard any unopened ones. Cover the mussels and keep to one side.

If using oysters, open them and remove the meat taking care to save the juice.

Very briefly simmer the oyster meats for about 2 minutes in their juice along with a very little white wine. Strain, reserving the juice. Keep warm.

In a pan quickly fry the mushrooms in butter. Keep warm.

Lay the sole fillets in a buttered ovenproof dish and pour the reserved liquid from the mussels or oysters over.

Season, dot with butter, and cook in a medium oven 190C/375F Gas 5 for 15 minutes until cooked but still firm.

Gently pour a little of the liquor from the sole into the velouté sauce. Just a little as you do not want a very runny sauce. Reheat the mussels or oysters and arrange them around the sole fillets. Add the mushrooms. Cover loosely with foil and keep warm.

Stir the sauce with a little added liquor until smooth and gently boil until thickened. In a bowl stir some of the cream into the yolks. Add some of the hot sauce, stirring until smooth. Return all of it to the pan. Add the rest of the cream, stir the sauce over a low heat until hot and thick but don't allow it to boil. Remove from the heat, check seasoning.

Pour some of the sauce over the fillets, mushrooms and mussels or oysters. Serve any remaining sauce separately.

Alternatively you can dish the fillets individually on plates with the mussels or oysters, mushrooms and sauce. Add a sprinkling of chopped parsley or scissored chives for colour and serve with a green salad and crusty bread to mop up the sauce.

Sole à la Bonne Femme

I wonder who the 'good' woman was! (In French, Bonne Femme means 'simple, good natured woman'). Perhaps it was because she served the sole quickly and simply in a 'no nonsense' way.

Sole à la Meunière

The Miller's wife too. It must have been that coating of flour and cooking in butter with a resulting crisp golden appearance that makes her so memorable.

Sole à la Fermière

Another wife. This time the Farmer's who no doubt used red wine to cook the sole. On serving, I'm sure the remaining red wine was not wasted.

These 3 recipes are all very simple using an unfilleted sole. Part of the pleasure is to sit coaxing the fish-meat away from the bone, enjoying each mouthful. These dishes are certainly to be lingered over.

Sole à la Bonne Femme and Sole à la Meunière are classic recipes that have been endorsed by Escoffier who believed that recipes should be simple so that the true flavour of the fish could be enjoyed.

Sole à la Bonne Femme

For two people, take two medium-sized soles. If desired, remove the dark skin from the upper side. Your fishmonger will probably do this for you. Leave the white underside.

Finely chop a small onion. Add 120g /4 oz mushrooms and scatter over the bottom of a heavy-duty iron or enamel dish. Fry in a little butter for 5 minutes.

Place the soles on top. Dot with butter, seasoning and lemon juice. Add a wineglass of white wine. Cover and cook in a medium oven 180C/350F Gas 4 for 10 minutes.

Meanwhile, on a plate, sprinkle 1 tbsp plain flour over 60g/2oz butter and mash it in with a fork. Add this in small dots around the fish. This will thicken and enrich the dish. Cook for a further 5 minutes.

To give a more golden colour, flash under a very hot grill.

Place the fish on two plates, give the onion and mushroom mixture a good stir, adding a drop more wine if necessary. Serve with the fish.

Alternatively this recipe can be prepared using a large frying pan. Turn once during cooking.

Sole à la Meunière

For two people, take two medium sized soles.

Remove the dark skin as explained on Page 20.

Lightly coat the sole with seasoned flour.

Use clarified butter to cook the fish in.

Clarified butter can be heated to a higher temperature without burning and has a purer smell of butter.

To clarify the butter, bring 120g/4 oz gently to the boil. Boil for a minute, set aside to cool and settle. Strain the butter through a muslin cloth or very fine nylon sieve so that the white solids are removed.

Fry the fish in the butter until golden brown on both sides. Place on a serving dish. An extra swirl of butter in the pan and onto the fish would give that final flourish.

Sole à la Fermière

For two people take two medium sized soles.
In a small frying pan, fry a finely chopped onion, and 120g/4 oz sliced mushrooms. Add a scattering of herbs, such as parsley and thyme.
Lay the soles in a buttered ovenproof dish. Dot them with butter, season and pour over.
180ml/6 fl oz red wine.
Cook in a medium oven 190C/375F, Gas 5 for 10 minutes.
While the fish is cooking, on a plate mash 60g/2oz butter with 1 level tbsp plain flour.
When the sole are cooked, serve them on two plates.
Strain the juice from the ovenproof dish into the frying pan. Add the mashed butter and a little more red wine if necessary. When bubbling, add the herb, mushroom and onion mixture. Spoon around the fish.

SPRAT

Sprat	*Sprattus sprattus*
Guernsey French	*d'la M'nise sardaine* (f)
Jersey French	*êprot, esprot* (m)
French	*sprat*

The sprat is a member of the herring family. It grows to about 14 cms long. It looks more like a sardine than a herring as it is much paler in colour. It has a ridge of spiny scales along the belly.

It lives in large shoals in all the northern oceans and is found as far south as the Mediterranean.

In some countries, fresh sprats are very popular, while in other countries, they aren't given a second glance.

Sprats are smoked and canned and are known as Sild and Brisling. They are delicious to eat. There is no waste as canning softens the bones and every morsel may be eaten.

The canned fish can be mashed and used as a very tasty sandwich filling.

Smoked sprats can be eased off the bone and used in hors d'oeuvre with lemon juice squeezed over.

Fresh sprats can be tossed in flour and fried whole.

~   ~   ~

SAND-EEL

Green or Greater Sand-Eel	*Hyperoplus sp.*
Smooth or 'red' sandeel	*Gymnammodytes semisquamatus*
The Lesser Sand Eel	*Ammodytes tobianus*
Guernsey French	*Vert lanchon* – greater sand-eel (m)
	Lanchon d'la catte – lesser sand-eel (m)
Jersey French	*Lanchon* (m), *louache pus grand* (f) – greater sand-eel
	Maidre or moindre lanchon (m) – lesser
French	*Lançon* (m) and *équille* (f)

The most common sand-eels in Bailiwick waters are the greater sand-eel which grows up to 40 cms long and the 'red' or smooth sand-eel which grows up to 20 cms long. The Greater sandeel swims in great shoals out at sea, while the 'red' sand-eel is the inshore species. Another name for the inshore sand-eel is sand lance. The name 'lance' is apt as they can bury themselves more than 30 cms/ 12inches in the sand. There they can stay for several hours. At sea, they are caught in nets.

Sand-eels can also be dug, or raked in sandy bays around the coast. There was a vogue for sand-eeling like this when I was a child and it would become a great adventure as it always seemed to happen at night in brilliant moonlight. Armed with garden forks, a party of us would set out to a suitable beach. Digging down with our forks, the eels would be disturbed and would jump around with great agility. This led to much darting around by us to try to catch them. It was great fun as well as a free meal too, very tasty and nutritious. The catch tended to be cooked on the spot and was sometimes 'stretched' with a few rashers of bacon in the pan – the original 'Surf and Turf'! If you see sand-eels in the Market, do try them. They are quick and easy to prepare, children love them too.

The best way to cook them is to cut off the head, dragging the innards out very gently. If they are on the small side, leave them whole.

Toss them in flour and fry in hot oil or clarified butter till crisp and golden. Serve with wedges of lemon and crusty bread.

TURBOT

Turbot	*Psetta maxima*
Guernsey french	*turbot* (m)
Jersey french	*turbot* (m)
French	*turbot* (m)

A large flatfish. It has a deeper, more rounded body than the halibut and is smaller. It is a browny sandy colour with small darker nodules on its upper side. The underside is white. It grows to 80 cms.

It lives on the seabed in deep water. Younger ones may be found closer inshore.

It is caught mainly in the North Sea and is available all year round. It is an expensive fish, often considered the 'Prince' of flatfish.

It is sold in fillets, steaks or as a whole fish. A small turbot is known as a 'Chicken' Turbot. .

The turbot's flesh is white and it is often poached to retain the whiteness.

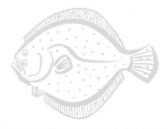

Turbot with Pink Peppercorns

There is a variety of pink peppercorns available. They can be dried or bottled in brine. For this recipe, I use those in brine.

Serves 4
4 turbot steaks, each weighing approx 180g/6oz
3 teaspoonfuls of brined peppercorns
150 ml / 5 fl oz or small carton double cream
150ml / 5 fl oz white wine
120g /4oz butter
30g/1oz flour

Turbot is one fish that is always delivered gutted, which can be a relief!

Gently crush the peppercorns in a pestle.

Brush the turbot steaks with a little butter. Press the crushed peppercorns onto each side of the turbot steaks.

In a thick-bottomed frying pan, melt the butter until almost smoking. Add the turbot steaks, keep them moving so they don't stick. Lower the heat and cook for 3 or 4 minutes. Turn and cook the other side. If you have a ridged frying pan the steaks look really good.

Remove and keep warm.

Add the plain flour to the buttery mixture in your pan and mix until smooth. Add the white wine and gradually bring to boiling point. If using a ridged pan, rinse the buttery mixture with the white wine into a small pan, add the flour and mix well. If the sauce is too thick, add a little more wine.

Remove from heat, add the cream and mix until smooth. Reheat but do not boil.

Serve individually on warmed plates, with a little of the sauce carefully poured over.

Serve the remaining sauce separately.

Turbot with Red Cabbage

Serves 4
4 turbot steaks each weighing approx. 180g/6 oz
1 tbsp chopped thyme
4 bay leaves
30g /1 oz butter
275ml / 10 fl oz made up of half water and half wine
150ml/5 fl oz double cream
Chives for garnish
Half a red cabbage

1 onion	275ml/10fl oz cider
1 large bramley apple	Salt and pepper
6 juniper berries	60g/ 2 oz butter

The red cabbage can be prepared well in advance.

In an ovenproof casserole, place the finely shredded cabbage, the sliced apple, sliced onion and crushed juniper berries. Season with salt and pepper. Pour over the cider. Cook in a moderate oven 100C/ 375 F Gas 5 for about 2 hours, turning occasionally. Aim to have very little liquid left.

Place the turbot steaks in a buttered ovenproof dish. Scatter a little lemon thyme on each steak and dot each with a generous piece of butter. Place a bay leaf on the butter. Season. Just cover with the water and wine, or fish stock if you have it.

Cook in a moderate oven for 20 minutes. Remove fish and keep warm.

In a small saucepan, reduce the cooking liquor until you have about 3 tbsp. Remove from heat and then add 150ml/5 fl oz cream to make the sauce.

Before serving the red cabbage, add the butter. This makes the cabbage look rich and glossy.

Serve a piece of turbot on each plate. Snip some chives on each, then place a generous pile of red cabbage alongside. Finally pour the sauce gently over and around the fish.

WHITEBAIT

Whitebait	*Clupeidae* (small herring fishes)
Guernsey French	*d'la v'nise* (f)
Jersey French	*d'la v'nîse*
French	*Jeunes harengs* (m) or *blanchaille* (f)

Whitebait is the fry of the herring.

It is available February to July

Whitebait needs very little preparation but should be eaten as soon as cooked. Left even five minutes it will begin to loose its crispness and if kept warm will become soggy and greasy.

All that needs to be done is to rinse and thoroughly dry the whitebait with absorbent kitchen paper. Toss in a bag of seasoned flour.

To cook, they can be deep or shallow fried using sunflower oil. It should be heated until almost smoking. A minute or two of cooking is long enough for them to become golden and crisp.

Serve immediately with wedges of lemon.

If you prefer a spicier taste a teaspoonful of curry powder can be added to the seasoned flour.

The average serving of whitebait as a starter would be 120g/4oz per person.

For a main course 250g/8oz per person would be recommended.

~   ~   ~

WHITING/POLLACK

Pollack   *Pollachius pollachius*
Whiting   *Merlangius merlangus*
Guernsey French *Lu* (m) – used in the higher parishes
                 Liotin (m) – used in the lower parishes
Jersey French   *Lieu* (m)
French   *merlan* – whiting
                 lieu jaune – pollock
The patois name is the same for both species

Channel Islanders tend to regard whiting and pollack as the same fish, using either name when buying it. In fact, whiting is far less common than pollack. Invariably it is pollack that is caught. It is plentiful around the islands, a favourite area being around wrecks where they are caught using lines.

Both are members of the cod family.

Whiting has a blue/green back with silvery sides and belly and a darkish stripe down the side of its body from head to tail. It has a dark spot behind the pectoral fin or gill. The smooth skin needs very little scaling.

Whiting grows to 40cm/16 inches but the average size is 30 cms/ 12 inches.

There is also the Blue whiting which is found in much deeper water.

Whiting flesh is very delicate and a little difficult to handle. It also has the reputation of being 'invalid food' as the sweet small flakes are easily digested.

I am told that there is nothing better than a winter-caught whiting.

Pollack looks more like cod because of its dark back, yellowish gold sides and creamy belly. Its lower lip protrudes beyond the upper and it has no barbel. Pollack also need very little in the way of scaling. It is a much bigger fish than whiting. Average size is 50 cms/ 20 inches and it is found in deeper water.

As well as around the islands, both whiting and pollack are found in shoals around Britain and the Atlantic and are available all year round but are best from August to March.

Both whiting and pollack are very versatile and the simpler the cooking the better. They can be cooked whole, filleted or as cutlets.

Fried Fillets of Whiting/Pollack with Parsley Sauce

Serves 4
4 fillets approx. 180g/6 oz
2tbsp olive oil

30g/1oz butter
Flour for coating
Salt and pepper

Rinse and pat dry. Coat with seasoned flour.

Heat oil and butter and fry until golden each side.

For parsley sauce see page 207.

~   ~   ~

Baked fillets of Whiting/Pollack with Caper Sauce

This is a useful recipe for a supper party as the fish can be cooked in the oven and the sauce finished just before serving. Make sure the sauce is green and runny as it looks really attractive on and around the fish.

Place the fillets in a roasting pan or ovenproof dish into a moderate oven just as people are about to begin their first course. By the time they have finished and the plates have been cleared, the fish is cooked. Just the sauce needs to be finished.

Serves 4
4 fillets approx. 180g/ 6oz
Sauce
1 heaped tbsp capers
275 ml/10 fl oz dry white wine
90g/3oz butter

30g/1oz flour
2 tbsp chopped parsley
A scattering of any fresh herb
  you might have at hand
Salt and pepper
Juice of 1 lemon

Lightly butter the roasting pan or oven-proof dish then add the washed and dried fillets, with a piece of butter on each one. Season and sprinkle with chopped fresh herbs and capers. Pour around the white wine and lemon juice, cover with foil.

Bake in a moderate oven 200C/400F, Gas 6 for 15 minutes.

Meanwhile melt the remaining butter in a saucepan, add the flour and mix until smooth.

When the whiting is cooked, remove it from the oven and keep warm. Gently pour the cooking liquid, including the capers and the chopped herbs, into the saucepan with the melted butter and flour. Mix until smooth, adding more wine if necessary. Slowly bring to the boil. Add the parsley and check the seasoning.

Place a fillet on each plate. Cover generously with the sauce.

A bowl of small boiled potatoes and a green vegetable such as spinach would go well. To perfect the spinach, add a good dollop of crème fraîche and a grating of nutmeg.

Whiting/Pollack with Anchovy and Tomato

Serves 4
4 fillets approx 180g/6 oz each
Half tin anchovy fillets
1tsp capers
2tbsp tomato purée

2tbsp lemon juice
1tsp chopped lemon thyme
Olive oil
Pepper
White wine or water

In a pestle, pound the drained anchovy fillets, adding a little of the oil. Use more anchovies if you like a really strong flavour. Aim for a thick consistency. Add the tomato purée, lemon thyme, ground black pepper until you get a spreadable consistency. If too thick add a little more olive oil.

Spread the pollack/whiting fillets on both sides with the anchovy mixture. Lay in an ovenproof earthenware dish. Cover with cling film and leave to refrigerate for several hours.

Butter an ovenproof dish and lay the anchovied fillets in it. Scatter each fillet with breadcrumbs. Pour around 2 tbsp water or white wine and 2 tbsp of lemon juice. Season. Cover with foil. Bake in a moderate oven, 190C/375F Gas 5 for 10 minutes. Remove the foil and cook for a further 5 minutes.

Serve with a casserole of Pommes Anna (thinly sliced potatoes and onion layered with salt and black pepper with 150ml/5 fl oz cream and cooked in a moderate oven for 30/40 minutes). Also serve a green vegetable that is in season.

Whole Pollack with Herb Mayonnaise

Pollack lends itself to being cooked whole and served cold. It has a delicate flaky flesh which firms up on cooling.

Serves 4
A pollack weighing approx $1\frac{1}{2}$ kilos/3lbs
1 lemon
Salt and pepper
Olive oil
Herb Mayonnaise - See page 211.

The pollack can be cooked as you would a whole salmon in foil in a roasting pan.

Lay the cleaned fish on foil. Pour over a little olive oil, a scattering of herbs and the lemon juice. Season with salt and pepper and wrap carefully. Place the wrapped fish in a roasting tin.

Add a little water so that it does not stick (you don't want to tear the foil and lose the juices).

Cook it in a moderate oven for about 45 minutes.

Check that it is cooked by carefully teasing back the foil and inserting a knife to see if the flesh comes away from the bone easily.

Carefully remove the wrapped fish from the roasting pan and allow to cool.

When cool enough to handle, make a little opening and drain the juices into a bowl which can be saved (and possibly frozen) for later use.

Now allow the fish to thoroughly cool and firm up.

Serve with your favourite salads. Perhaps a potato salad topped with crispy fried bits of bacon and a chopped hard boiled egg.

WOLF-FISH

Wolf-Fish	*Anarhichas lupus*
Guernsey French	*vras*
French	*loup de mer*

This unattractive fish is also known as marine or ocean catfish.

It can be a metre long. It has a flattend blunt head rather resembling a cat with its ears laid back ready to pounce. Its wide, fleshy, lipped jaw has strong jagged teeth at the front and flattened grinding teeth at the back. It lives on crustaceans, molluscs and sea urchins. As a result of its diet, the flesh is pink. It tends to be sold skinned.

Wolf-fish with Courgettes and Tomatoes

Serves 4
750g/1½ lb piece of wolf-fish
or two fillets of the same weight
3 medium courgettes
500g/ 1lb tomatoes
1 lemon

60g/2 oz butter
1 onion
2 tbsp sunflower oil
1 tbsp lemon thyne
2 cloves garlic
Salt and pepper

Slice the onion amd garlic and fry in the butter for 5 minutes. Add the sliced courgettes and cook for a further 5 minutes. Finally add the chopped tomatoes and cook until mushy. Season with salt and pepper and scatter with lemon thyme. Place all in an ovenproof dish and keep warm.

Fry the fillets in sunflower oil until cooked and golden. Arrange the fillets on the vegetables. Pour the lemon juice over and around the fish.

If using a whole piece of fish, fry it in the sunflower oil until golden brown. Place it with the vegetables and pour the lemon juice around. Cover with foil and cook in a medium oven 200C/ 400F Gas 6 for about 20 minutes. Longer for a whole piece. Check that it is cooked. Serve with mashed potato and broad beans in a parsley sauce.

WRASSE

Wrasse	*Labridae sp*
Guernsey French	*vra* (m), *eune perlée* (f)
Jersey French	*vra* (m)
	coucou (m) – striped wrasse
	couotheux (m) – large ballan wrasse
French	*labre* (m)

Wrasse is a large and colourful group. Affectionately known as a 'rocky' or 'rockfish' but not to be confused with Rockling. The ballan wrasse and cuckoo wrasse are familiar names in these waters. They are found close in along the coast and rocky outcrops. They can grow up to 43cms / 17 inches. They have a heavy head, thick lips and a body covered with large brown / green scales.

There is a smaller wrasse, called Goldsinney which grows up to 18cms / 8 inches It lives on steep weed-covered rocks and is a favourite with anglers.

Wrasse always looks attractive on the fishmonger's slab because of its rich blue / orange / gold colour. Perhaps it reminds us of Mediterranean holidays or maybe it is just its brightness that attracts us.

It tends to be sold whole. Scaling is necessary and the fish can be filleted depending on how you plan to cook it.

Grilling, frying, barbecueing or baking in the oven are all good ways of cooking wrasse.

My favourite way to enjoy wrasse is to bake it and eat it cold, with mayonnaise.

Marie-Rose's Fish Soup

I am including this soup recipe here, because it is another great way to enjoy wrasse and, perhaps more importantly, because it reminds me of Marie-Rose, a friend of ours long ago in Casablanca who kindly made the soup for us and gave me the recipe. It is a deliciously rich pink soup.

For 6 people
1 kg/2 lbs of mixed fish but it is important to include a wrasse and two small red mullet

1 litre fish stock	2 glasses white wine (275ml /10 fl oz)
2 leeks	2 bay leaves
1 fennel bulb	1 tbsp chopped parsley
2 onions	Salt and pepper
3 plump cloves of garlic	A good pinch of saffron strands
500g /1lb ripe tomatoes	or half sachet of powdered saffron
Olive oil	150ml / 5 fl oz cream

If using the saffron filaments, soak them in a teacup of hot water for at least 30 minutes.

Sweat the roughly chopped onions, leeks, fennel and garlic in olive oil until soft, about 10 minutes. Remove and keep warm.

In the same pan add the gutted and cleaned and chopped up fish. Don't chop the fish too much as the pieces will be difficult to remove later on, (chunks rather than pieces).

Let them brown a little in olive oil. Now add the onions, garlic, leeks, fennel, and the chopped tomatoes. Finally the bay leaf and parsley and 2 glasses of white wine and fish stock to cover. Finally add the saffron water, filaments too. If using powder, sprinkle over. Season and gently simmer for 20 minutes. Don't overcook the soup or it will become bitter.

Strain into a sieve or mouli. Pick out as many of the bones from the fish as possible.

Carefully sieve or mouli the fish and vegetables.

Put the soup into the rinsed pan, taste for seasoning and adjust if necessary.

Just before serving, bring to the boil and off the boil, add 150ml/ 5 fl oz of double cream.

Fish soups are usually served with slices of toasted french bread and a rich sauce called rouille, for recipe see page 213.

Shellfish

What a rich abundance is found in our waters!

Shellfish is a large group which divides into two sections: Crustaceans and Molluscs.

CRUSTACEANS: *Include crabs, lobsters and prawns.*

MOLLUSCS *include gastropods that have a single shell such as ormers and limpets. Bivalves, such as scallops, mussels and clams, have two more or less the same sized hinged shells.*

CEPHALOPODS, *such as squid and cuttlefish, carry their shell within them.*

LOBSTER

Lobster	*Homarus vulgaris*
Guernsey French	*houmard* or *houmar* (m),
	une houmarde (a hen)
Jersey French	*honmard* (m)
French	*homard* (m)

Lobsters are found in deep water around our islands. All in their natural state are a rich blue/black colour but then on cooking turn red. They are caught all year round. When choosing one, take the body between finger and thumb and gently squeeze it. It should be firm, if it is loose, it could mean a recent body/shell change.

You will notice that it has two uneven claws which at the fishmonger's are tied or rubber-banded for safety's sake.

Because of the way the segments of the lobster are joined, it can only move backwards. When changing their shell they are especially vulnerable so tend to hide in rocky crevices with only the tips of their claws showing.

An ideal size is between about 1 kg/2lbs.

~   ~   ~

Lobster Bisque

Why waste a lobster on soup?

In fact, this is not only a classic but also an incomparable way of enjoying lobster. It makes the very best use of this sought after shellfish.

Serves 4

One live or cooked lobster weighing not more than 750g /1 $\frac{1}{2}$lbs

At the same time, ask the fishmonger for some bones (not from an oily fish) to make fish stock, see page 206.

1 small onion or two shallots	60g/ 2 oz flour
1 medium carrot	55ml/ 2 fl oz brandy
1 stalk of celery	260m/ 8fl oz white wine
120g /4oz butter	Small bunch parsley/2 tbsp chopped
Juice of half a lemon	1 litre fish stock
3 bay leaves	130 ml /4fl oz double cream
1 blade mace	Salt and pepper

Prepare the fish stock in readiness. You will need 1 litre.

If using a live lobster, cook it first – see page 21.

Cut the cooked lobster tail into pieces. Cut the carapace or body in half. Remove the intestinal cord and sack of grit. If there is coral, remove it along with the creamy liver and set to one side. Crack the claws. Remove the meat from the body, tail and claws and put to one side. Keep the larger pieces of shell.

Chop the onion or shallots, celery and carrot. Soften in half the butter in a large saucepan. Add the lobster meat, wine and brandy. Cover the lobster and vegetables with 1 litre of fish stock. Add the mace and bay leaf, season with salt and freshly ground black pepper.

Simmer for 20 minutes.

Strain the soup. Return the liquid to the pan. Add the larger pieces of shell, bring back to the boil and simmer for 15 minutes.

Meanwhile mash the liver and coral (if any) together.

Remove the soup from the heat and strain it to remove the pieces of shell.

Reserve a little of the meat. Whizz the remaining meat and vegetables in a blender, adding a little of the soup. Keep an eye open for any bits of shell that got away!

Chop the reserved meat.

Place the remaining half of the butter in the saucepan, add the flour and stir till smooth. Gradually add the blended mixture, the rest of the soup and the lemon juice. Bring slowly to the boil.

Whisk in the coral/liver mixture and stir in half the chopped meat.

Remove from the heat.

Stir in the cream. Sprinkle with the remaining reserved chopped lobster and chopped parsley.

Stir once and serve.

Lobster Mayonnaise

Somehow cold lobster lends itself to lunch whereas hot lobster seems more of an evening dish.

A lobster mayonnaise and chilled bottle of Chablis or Muscadet, al fresco, are summer delights – all that is needed is to get all the ingredients together at the same time, including good weather.

A good guide is 250/300g or 8/10oz of lobster in the shell per person. Alternatively, half a lobster per person.

Remove the claws. Lay the lobster belly up. With a sharp knife cut through the head on down through the body, continue through the tail so that you have two halves.

Remove the grey vein or spinal chord and the stomach sac.

Carefully crack the claws.

Remove the meat from the tail and body. Keep any coral and the liver (tomalley) separately.

Cut the lobster meat into small chunks and mix with a little mayonnaise.

Put the lobster meat in the halved shells. The claws can be arranged in such a way to make an attractive presentation.

The coral and tomalley can be mashed and added to a little mayonnaise and served in a small bowl. Another bowl of mayonnaise with perhaps some chopped parsley, gherkins and capers. Don't forget pickers to entice any meat tucked away in the body.

Lobster Mayonnaise really is one of the best al fresco meals.

With a blender, mayonnaise is quickly made. See page 211.

Lobster à l'Armoricaine

I have mulled over the words Amoricaine and Americaine. Armorique is an ancient word for Brittany and Armoricaine means ancient Breton. The word in Brittany used for America was Amorica. So is the dish an old Breton recipe or one created by a chef wanting to indulge his American clientele?

My ancestors were Breton and so my version is a Brittany one.

In testing my version, I was asked if I wanted a cock or hen lobster. I chose the hen and what a lucky choice that was. On adding the coral to the sauce, it became a rich speckled red, beautiful to look at and delicious to eat.

This recipe is suprisingly easy and really delicious.

Serves 4
2 freshly cooked lobsters approx 750g /1½ lbs each
750g/ 1½ lbs very ripe but firm tomatoes
60g/ 2 oz chopped onion
2 cloves garlic
150 ml /5 fl oz white wine
100ml/3 fl oz double cream
2 tbsp calvados
 425 ml/ 15 fl oz fish stock or 1 fish stock cube
30g/1 oz flour
90g/3oz butter
2 tbsp chopped parsley
Sprigs of thyme and rosemary
Salt and pepper

When buying the lobster, ask the fish-monger for some fish bones for the fish stock.

For 550 ml /20 fl oz stock use 500grms/1lb fish bones (not from oily fish such as herring or mackerel)

60g/2oz each of carrot, onion, celery - all chopped and a few sprigs of thyme and parsley. Cover bones and vegetables with 1 litre of water, simmer for 20 minutes, sieve and reduce till approximately half.

Alternatively use a fish stock cube.

Skin and peel the tomatoes by plunging them in boiling water for 2 or 3 minutes.

Remove the lobster claws. Take the tails with the underneath facing up and cut down the middle. Remove the intestinal veins which runs the whole length. Remove the meat and cut into chunks.

Cut the bodies in half, removing the stomach sacs and anything you don't like the look of. Scrape the creamy livers or tomalley onto a saucer along with any coral. Remove the meat.

Crack the claws and remove the meat.

Cut the emptied shells into fairly large pieces.

In a large frying pan or cast iron casserole, sweat the chopped onion and garlic in 60g/2 oz butter for 4 to 5 minutes. Add the chopped up lobster, including the larger pieces of shell. Raise the heat. Add the calvados and shake the pan.

Now add the tomatoes, wine, stock, herbs and seasoning. Cover and when just simmering, cook for 10 minutes. Remove from the heat.

Take out the lobster meat and shell, discarding the shell. Let the sauce reduce by half.

As the sauce reduces, mash the liver (tomalley) and coral with the remaining butter and 30g/1 oz of flour.

Return the lobster meat to the sauce. Gradually stir in the liver (tomalley) /coral butter mixture until well distributed and thickened. When hot, remove from the heat, stir in the cream, scatter with parsley and serve. Voila. Hommard à l'Armoricaine!

CRAB

Crab	*Cancer pagurus*
Guernsey French	*crabe* or *chancresse* (f), *chancre* (m)
Jersey French	*crabe* (f), *chancre* (m), *houais* (m)
French	*crabe* or *torteau* (m)

For me, this is what Guernsey is all about. It is my favourite food.

For centuries, chancres, spiders and green shore crabs were a common food for all Channel Islanders. No need for a fishing boat either. At low tide men would go down to the beaches in pairs. Holes were jealously guarded. Years ago, my husband was invited to go crabbing at the Creux Mahé by a fisherman. My husband couldn't help being reminded of meerkats – a man would pop up, have a look round and duck down, then another would pop up, have a look round and duck down. The 'look out' was on the alert for any approaching 'predator'! Whereabouts of holes would be handed down from father to son.

The body of a chancre can grow up to 25cms/10 inches across. (The minimum size for catching crabs is 14 cms/$5\frac{1}{2}$ inches). The shell or body is pinky brown with scalloped edges. The chancre has two large claws and four pairs of legs. They live on the rocky seabed, migrating to deeper water in winter.

They are available all year round. A mature female crab is at her best for eating during December and January when the eggs are inside her body.

Winter crabs are tastier. Maybe it is the very cold water that improves the flavour.

Crab can be eaten hot or cold but tends to be served cold.

Some people seem reluctant to 'pick' a crab. It just takes time, a good half-hour or more, so turn the radio on.

I'm told that an experienced crab-picker can pick one in three minutes!

Assemble what you need. Newspaper, two bowls, a chopping board, strong knife, hammer, crab picker and teaspoon.

First of all remove the legs and claws.

Having removed the legs and claws, hold the body or carapace firmly in the palm of your hand, underside uppermost. Remove the flap. Grasp the underbody using the holes from the legs for a really firm grip. Gently ease the top outer shell and underbody apart, this will need a good tug. When seperated remove the gills (spidery like fronds known as dead men's fingers) and discard them.

Now we are ready to empty the crab.

In one bowl empty the brown meat from the body. In the other goes all the white meat from the body, claws and legs.

Using a strong knife, cut the body into small pieces. Specific cuts are needed to get at the body meat otherwise a lot is wasted. This is the slowest part of the operation.

Now tackle the legs leaving the claws to last as these are easy and very rewarding. Break each leg into three at the joints, discarding the pointed tip. With the hammer or nutcrackers crack the pieces and using the picker, extract the meat. Finally the claws. Break them into three pieces at the joint. Using the hammer, crack the pieces and take out the meat.

Now you have two bowls of sweet smelling meat.

The shell can be used to present the crab. Wash and dry it with paper towel, smearing the inside with oil.

Served this way, it is an attractive focal point and can be decorated with salad leaves or herbs surrounding it.

Alternatively, the brown meat can be placed in a wedge down the middle of the shell with the white meat either side.

Serve with a bowl of mayonnaise or tartare sauce, lots of crusty bread and new potatoes tossed in mint and parsley. Along with a chilled bottle of white wine, the crab becomes the focal point of the meal or should I say – a feast.

Crab can also be served hot in the following ways.

~   ~   ~

Crab cakes

For 4 people
500g/ 1 lb cooked crabmeat 90g/3oz white breadcrumbs
1 small onion
60g/ 2oz butter   Tabasco
2 eggs   1 tbsp chopped coriander
1 lemon   1 tbsp chopped parsley
salt, pepper   Oil and butter for frying

Fry the finely chopped onion in the butter until it is soft but not brown. Remove from the heat.

In a bowl mix the crabmeat, breadcrumbs, cooled onion, egg yolks, lemon juice, chopped coriander and parsley. Season with salt and pepper and a few drops of tabasco.

Whisk the egg whites until stiff. Gently fold into the crab mixture and form into eight cakes.

Place in the fridge for at least two hours to settle and firm up.

Fry in a mixture of oil and butter, 30g/1oz butter and 1 tbsp oil for 5 minutes on each side. Don't turn until a firm crust has formed as they are delicate and can fall apart.

Crab Soufflé

Serves 4

250g/8oz of cooked crabmeat	275 ml /10fl oz milk
4 eggs	1 tsp curry powder
1 small onion	30g/1 oz grated Parmesan cheese
60g/2oz butter	(or other hard cheese)
60g/2oz plain flour	Salt and pepper

In a saucepan, fry the finely chopped onion in the butter until softened. Add the flour and curry powder and mix until smooth. Add the milk gradually until you have a fairly thick creamy sauce.

Separate the eggs. Add the egg yolks, half the grated Parmesan and finally the crabmeat. Mix gently, not to break up the crab meat too much. Season.

About 40 minutes before you serve the soufflé, whisk the egg whites until stiff. Fold into the crab mixture and turn into a buttered soufflé dish or ovenproof dish. Sprinkle the remaining Parmesan on top.

Bake in a hot oven 200C/400F Gas 6 for 25-30 minutes.

After 25 minutes carefully test with a knife if it comes out with mixture sticking to it, bake for 5 minutes longer, unless you like a creamy middle.

Serve with a green salad. Alternatively, green and red peppers that have been sweated with an onion in olive oil and seasoned with a sprinkling of ground cumin and coriander, salt and pepper. Courgettes could be used instead of peppers.

Crab Pancakes

Serves 6
120g/4oz plain flour
2 eggs
275ml/10fl oz milk and water mixed
2 tbsp melted butter

Filling
Approx 360g/12 oz cooked crab meat
1 egg
1tbsp chopped parsley
1tbsp chopped coriander
1 tsp chopped lemon thyme
1 tsp soy or Worcestershire sauce
A few drops tabasco
Juice of half a lemon
Salt and pepper

First make the pancakes. These can be made an hour or so in advance.

Crack the eggs into a bowl and whisk until light and frothy. Whisk in the flour adding a little of the milk and water until smooth. Leave to rest for as long as possible, at least 30 minutes.

This quantity should make 12 pancakes.

Just before making them, add 2 tbsp melted butter to the batter, this makes them crispy and greasing the pan is not necessary, except for the first one.

When made, cover and keep warm.

Place the crabmeat in a bowl. Add all the ingredients and mix lightly. Divide into 12 and place a portion down the centre of each pancake. Roll and place in a rectangular earthenware dish, two layers if necessary. Cover with foil and reheat in a moderate oven for 15/20 minutes.

Serve with an additional sprinkling of parsley and a spicy tomato sauce or a sauce of your choice poured over the pancakes or served separately.

Crab Soup

Serves 4

A good pinch of saffron threads or half teaspoon of powdered saffron

1 small cooked crab	150ml/ 5 fl oz double cream
1 carrot	chives
1 onion	1 tbsp olive oil
1 leek	cayenne pepper
2 potatoes	salt

Place the saffron strands in a teacup and cover with boiling water. Leave to infuse for about 20 minutes.

Having picked the crab, put the bigger pieces of shell in a pan with a handful of fresh or scattering of dried herbs. Cover with water. Simmer for 20 minutes, strain and keep to one side. Discard the shell. This is the stock but if you are using ready picked crab meat make a court bouillon or use a fish-stock cube.

In the rinsed pan, gently fry the finely chopped carrot, leek and onion in 1 tbsp olive oil. Add the chopped potatoes. Cover with the stock. Add the saffron liquid including the strands. If using powdered, sprinkle on top. Cover and simmer for 20 minutes until the vegetables are cooked.

Add the crab meat and allow to simmer for 2 or 3 minutes. Whizz in the blender, food processor or mouli. Return to the pan and if too thick add a little water or white wine.

Before serving, bring slowly to the boil. Remove from the heat. Stir in the cream and sprinkle with scissored chives and a dusting of cayenne pepper.

Serve with a generous bowl of croûtons that have been fried in olive oil in a pan that has been well rubbed with garlic.

Or as with fish soup, slices of french bread that have been slightly toasted and served with rouille. See page 212.

~   ~   ~

SPIDER CRAB

Spider crab	*Maja brachydactylus*
Guernsey French	*paincllos, haeu'lin, houblin, heuvlin*
Jersey French	*pihangne* (f), *hueûlîn* (m)
French	*Araignée de mer*

The spider crab is also known as the spiny crab. It has long, spider-like legs and two small claws. The mature male has bigger claws than the female. It uses its long legs to camouflage itself by covering its body with bits of seaweed as it hides in rocky crevices. During the early spring, spider crabs congregate, forming a heap on the seabed. This heap moves all the time, the bottom ones climbing to the top. As this happens the female disperses her eggs into the sea. Once this has happened, the 'spiders' move away and won't be seen in any great numbers until April and May.

A fisherman tells me that a Christmas Spider is the best. Those caught at this time of the year are found in deep water.

The colour of spider crabs ranges from reddish orange to brown. When cooked they are bright red.

'Spider' is a favourite with Channel Islanders. When in season and plentiful this was a regular meal. Spiders are cheap, sweet-tasting and very nutritious. All one needs is an old newspaper, a hammer, crab picker and dish. Often not even a dish is needed, the meat from the crab being eaten as it is removed from the body and legs. Bread and butter, a bottle of vinegar and a large pot of tea accompanied the meal.

Vinegar has always been a favourite accompaniment for spiders as it 'cuts' the richness of the meat. One spider per person is normal. The meat is in the legs though the body is still worth picking.

A few years ago, I remember a lady being taken in by the colour of a spider she had bought. She took it back to the fishmonger explaining that there was something wrong with it. (She unwrapped it and I remember seeing a grey, runny, soggy mess.)

As kindly as possible, the fishmonger explained that she hadn't cooked it! Spider is cooked and prepared in the same way as a chancre.

CRAYFISH

Salt Water Crayfish	*Palinuras elephas*
Guernsey French	*crabe à co* (m)
Jersey French	*crabe à co* (m)
French	*langouste* (f)

Crayfish is also known as spiny lobster. It can also be called crawfish. There is also the freshwater crayfish. All in all, quite a lot of confusion.

The crayfish is related to the lobster. It is best from April to October.

The crayfish/spiny lobster is a rare delight. I am told it is making its way back into our waters. Unfortunately its scarcity has pushed prices up so much that it has become a luxury. However, there is very little waste when dealing with a crayfish.

The flavour is something special being sweet like lobster but the ivory fibrous flesh has more bite to it.

It has a rough spiny body with two large horns to protect its eyes and two long antennae. It has five pairs of legs but no claws. It is a rich, rusty, red-brown colour and on cooking, turns reddy/pink like the lobster. They grow to about 50 cm/ 20 inches and are caught in pots.

Crayfish and lobster recipes can be interchanged.

A good guide for quantity is about 500g/1lb (including shell) per person.

Cooking crayfish/spiny lobster is the same as cooking lobster – see page 21.

I know that they are a rarity but if you should see one and there is a special celebration, do try it. You will be richly rewarded.

After cooking the crayfish, allow it to cool and serve with homemade mayonnaise. Your favourite salads and of course only the best to wash it down – champagne!

Prawn

Prawn	*Palaemom serratus* of the *Palaemonidae* family
Guernsey french	*chevatte* (f)
Jersey French	*grôsse chèrvette* (f)
French	*crevette* (f)

There can be confusion over prawns and shrimps. The Americans tend to call both families shrimp, while Australians call them both prawns. Things can be further confused because the Dublin Bay prawn is really a Norway lobster!

The common prawn is what is found mainly around these waters. It likes a sandy seabed but there is also the deep-water or Northern prawn (*Pandalus borealis*).

There are very many species of prawns but the most common that we see at the fishmonger's is the deep-water prawn which comes from Icelandic and Norwegian waters. It is bigger than the common prawn. There is also the King prawn found in Spanish and Portuguese waters. Another is the Tiger prawn recognised by the dark stripes on its shell. It is imported from Indian and south-east Asian waters. Prawns imported from the Gulf and Far East lack flavour and are best used for hot or spicy dishes.

Frozen prawns are often 'glazed' which is supposed to prevent them dehydrating and getting freezer burn. The glaze is simply a layer of water, so when you choose them, ones with the least glaze are a better bet, weight-wise, otherwise you are just buying water.

Prawns can be bought in many different ways. There is a wide range to choose from:

Freshly cooked or cooked and frozen. With or without their heads. Shelled or unshelled. They are available all year round because of the huge, worldwide prawn fishing industry.

Cooking and shelling is quick and easy. Large prawns need to be deveined as the vein can contain sandy grit.

Servings will vary depending on the size of the prawn.

Allow 250g/8oz (with shells) or 120g/4oz (shelled) per person.

Cooking times are short. Drop them into boiling salted water, bring back to the boil for 1 minute. Drain and cool.

Prawns are immensely versatile and always a favourite. They can be eaten hot or cold. I feel that, as with crab and lobster, prawns taste better when eaten cold.

Cold, they can be served either shelled or unshelled with a bowl of mayonnaise, lots of bread and a green salad. Leaving the tail on is useful especially when you are dipping them in salsas and dips. They can be tossed in a herby vinaigrette or turned into a paste or potted with a layer of clarified butter. Prawn sauce goes with most fish, adding a pinky coral colour as well as its distinct shellfish flavour.

Served hot they can be curried or served in many oriental ways. They can be served in a sauce, in vol au vents, deep-fried, barbecued or grilled. Their versatility is endless.

Fried Prawns

Serves 4 people
500g/1 lb shelled (uncooked) prawns
60g /2oz butter
Clove garlic
1 small onion or 2 shallots
2 tbsp lemon juice
2 tbsp chopped flat parsley (if you have it, 1 tsp chopped lemon thyme)
Salt and cayenne pepper

In the butter, very gently fry the finely chopped onion and garlic. Add the prawns, heat through. Add the lemon juice, parsley and thyme. Season. Coat well and serve with spicy hot rice and wedges of lemon.

You can use this recipe using whole uncooked ones but you will need more, approximately 750g/1½ lbs. A little more butter and lemon juice too.

Add the prawns as they are (heads and shells and all) to the fried onion and garlic. Add the extra butter and lemon juice. Toss till a reddish brick colour.

Eating this way is a bit messy and takes a bit longer but is great fun and turns the meal into more of a feast.

 *Barbecued Prawns*

Delicious cooked over the barbecue, either on a skewer or fine wire grill.

Marinating the prawns beforehand is very important – the longer the better.

You may have your favourite mixture or you can start from scratch.

Buy uncooked prawns with the shell on, at least 6 per person (much will depend on the size).

Marinate them, shell and all, in a mixture of lemon juice, olive oil, cayenne pepper, salt, a few drops of tabasco and a couple of tablespoonfuls of tomato purée.

Alternatively, choose a Chinese mixture of soy sauce, finely chopped fresh ginger, rice wine vinegar and chopped fresh coriander. There are endless marinades and we each have our favourite.

When barbecuing, prawns need only a very short time, 30 seconds each side, otherwise they will become dry and chewy.

Even if they do get a bit charred, it is fun to sit and peel the charred shell – messy – but what is underneath is delicious.

Prawn Bisque

This is delicious and well worth the effort. The colour too is most appetising.

Serves 4
500g/1lb uncooked prawns
1 onion
1 carrot
1stick celery
1 medium potato
60g /2oz butter
100ml /3 fl oz double cream
Good pinch of saffron strands or half teaspoonful powdered saffron
Chives
800ml/ $1\frac{1}{2}$ pints fish stock
Salt and pepper

Place the strands of saffron in a teacup. Cover with boiling water and leave to infuse.

Shell and devein the prawns. Peel the potato and dice it along with the other vegetables. Fry all gently in the butter. Add the fish stock along with the chopped prawns.

Tie the prawn shells in muslin and add to the soup.

Season with salt pepper. Add the saffron. Simmer gently for 30 minutes.

Remove the shell and liquidise or sieve the soup. Make sure the soup is the consistency you like, add a little milk or fish stock if necessary.

Before serving, bring gently to the boil. Remove from the heat, stir in the cream and snip some chives on top.

Prawn Satay

Satay comes from Indonesia and Malaya. The meat or fish is always threaded on wooden sticks and the kebebs are cooked over charcoal. The traditional dip has a peanut base.

Serves 4
Work out how many prawns you think each person will eat. It is easier than buying by weight. 8 prawns per person is reasonable depending on the size.
Buy uncooked prawns as long as they are fresh. Alternatively, use frozen prawns.
2 limes

1 tbsp dark soy sauce	1 tsp powdered turmeric
30 g/1 oz creamed coconut	Chilli sauce or tabasco
1 tbsp runny honey	Salt and pepper

Shell the prawns. In a bowl, mix the creamed coconut, lime juice, soy sauce, honey, a few drops of chilli sauce or tabasco and turmeric, season with salt and pepper. Finally add the prawns and leave to marinate for about 2 hours.

Drain the prawns and carefully thread them on wooden satay sticks, having first soaked the sticks in water for at least 20 minutes.

Grill or barbecue the kebabs for two or three minutes. Drizzle a little of the marinade over them as they cook.

Boiled rice or noodles and stir-fry vegetables go well. Peanut sauce is tradtionally served with most satay recipes. (Peanut sauce – see page 211).

The above recipe can be used in the following way.

Instead of threading the prawns on kebab sticks, pour 1 tbsp oil in a wok. Throw in the prawns and the marinade. Push around till the prawns are cooked and the mixture bubbling.

Serve as they are or with noodles.

Prawn and Mushroom Tempura

Tempura is associated with Japan and was originally introduced to Europe by Portuguese missionaries. Only fish and vegetables were coated in the finest of batters and fried in vegetable oil. Now fruits such as strawberries or pineapple chunks can be dipped and fried in the same way.

Spicy sweet and sour dips are a favourite with tempura.

Serves 4
750g/1½ lbs fresh uncooked prawns with shells on
250g/ 8oz button mushrooms

Batter
120g/4 oz plain flour
2 eggs
150ml / 5 fl oz water
Salt and pepper

First make the batter. Separate the eggs, placing the yolks in a bowl. Reserve the whites. Add a little water to the yolks and mix thoroughly. Gradually add the flour mixing to a smooth thick consistency, adding water as necessary. Whisk the egg whites and gently fold in, leave to rest for 20 minutes.

Shell the prawns and devein if necessary. Wipe the mushrooms.

Heat the oil. Test temperature by dropping a little batter in, if it sizzles it is ready.

Dip the prawns in the batter and fry till golden brown. Do not overcrowd the pan but cook in batches. Lift out and drain on kitchen paper.

Dip the mushrooms and cook in the same way.

Serve with your favourite dip, something spicy with lime juice and ginger.

Brown Shrimp

Brown Shrimp	*Crangon crangon*
Guernsey French	*chervette* (f), small shrimp - *chervin* (m)
Jersey French	*chèrvette* (f), small shrimp - *chèrvîn* (m)
French	*crevette* (f)

The shrimp is similar to the prawn but much smaller, maximum length being 5 cm/2 inches. It has a much smaller antennae with a translucent look blending in very well with the sandy shallows and gullies it inhabits. It is the smallest crustacean to be caught and eaten in any quantity.

Shrimping is great fun to be enjoyed by children and adults alike. Trying to catch these tiny creatures as they dart hither and thither needs dexterity especially if enough for a 'feed' are to be caught.

Shrimp have a very defined taste of the sea. If you have the opportunity to catch some, cooking must be of the very minimum. Just plunge them into boiling salted water, bring back to the boil and drain.

Shelling can be done by either breaking the head and body apart and removing the shell from the tail, or keeping them whole and just removing the shell from the tail.

Shrimp Paste or Paté

Pastes used to be very popular as sandwich fillings but somehow the idea of fish paste reminds me of the leanness of the war and early post war years. The word paté or terrine seems better. In fact there is nothing better than a real homemade shrimp paste. This is also a good way of stretching shrimp as there is an addition of white fish.

To serve 4
120g /4oz cooked shelled shrimp and 120g /4oz white flaked fish – such as cod or haddock
180g /6oz butter
Grated nutmeg or pinch of mace
Cayenne

Cover the white fish with water and bring gently to the boil. Simmer for five minutes until cooked. Drain, saving the water.

Reserve half the shrimps. Blend or process the remaining half along with the fish, lemon juice, spice and seasoning. At the same time gradually pour in 120g/4oz melted butter. Blend till smooth, adding a little of the cooking liquid if too stiff.

Remove from the food processor and gently add the remaining half of shrimp. If they are large, it may be necessary to roughly chop them, otherwise leave them whole.

In ramekins or a bowl, pot, carefully pressing down.

Heat the remaining 60g/2oz butter, skim and carefully pour the clarified butter over the surface of the paste.

Use when thoroughly chilled.

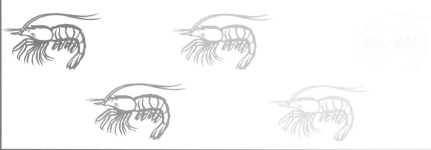

CLAM

There are many species. The most common are:
Carpet Shell Clam – *Venerupis decussata* – native to British waters.
In French – *Palourde*
Quahog – *Mercenaria mercenaria*, found in these waters but originally from the east coast of USA; it is also known as the Little neck. In French – *Praire.*
Warty venus – *Venus verrucosa*, native to British waters
There is also the small Manila clam which is imported and is ideal for pasta dishes.

Clams are available all year round and have been sucessfully farmed but, like all shellfish, are best during winter.

Clams can be eaten like oysters or cooked like mussels and are opened in the same way.

A simple way of helping them to open is to lower them into warm water – this makes them relax. Caught unawares, the knife goes in easily.

The meat can be used in hot dishes such as stuffed clams.

Stuffed Quahogs/clams - (praire)

Serves 4
6 clams/ quahogs per person
100g / 3oz mushrooms
60g / 2oz piece of bacon or rashers

60g /2oz fresh breadcrumbs
Salt and pepper
1 tbsp chopped parsley
2 tbsp grated Parmesan cheese

Open the quahogs by placing in a roomy saucepan with a little water to prevent them sticking. Over a high heat, cook, shaking continually until the shells are open. Discard any unopened ones. Remove the meat taking care not to break the hinge. You will need 8 shells per person. Put the meat to one side.

In a little butter or olive oil, fry the finely diced bacon. Add the finely chopped mushrooms. Cook two or three minutes. Add the bread crumbs, chopped parsley and seasoning.

Take 16 hinged shells and place a teaspoonful of stuffing in each half. Chop the quahogs and place a little on the stuffing, gently pressing down. Sprinkle a little grated Parmesan cheese and dot with butter.

Bake in a moderate oven 180C/350F, Gas 4 for 10-12 minutes until bubbling and golden brown. Alternatively, grill.

Serve on a bed of watercress or something similar. This will prevent them from capsizing and the colour is good against the shells

Carpet Shell Clam (palourde) with a White Wine Sauce

Serves 4
2 kilos /4lbs palourdes or carpet shell clams
1 medium onion
2 cloves garlic   Grated gruyère or Parmesan
30g/1 oz flour   275 ml /10 fl oz white wine
1 red and 1 green pepper   2 tbsp olive oil
1 tbsp freshly chopped coriander Salt and pepper

Open the clams by placing them in a roomy saucepan with a little water to prevent them sticking. Over a high heat, cook, shaking continually until all the shells are open. Discard any that remain closed.

Allow to cool, then remove the flesh.

Fry the chopped onion and garlic in 2 tbsps olive oil. Add the finely sliced peppers and fry until softened and collapsed. Sprinkle the flour over and gently mix in. Season. Add the white wine, lemon juice and chopped coriander and finally the clams.

Tip into an ovenproof dish and sprinkle liberally with the Parmesan cheese. Place under the grill until bubbling and golden brown.

Serve with plain boiled rice.

COCKLE

Cockle	*Cerastoderma edule*
French	*cocque* (m)

The cockle is the most common accessible 'clam' found in our waters. Their shells are brown, pale yellow or off-white and are joined at the base. Their maximum size is about 6 cm across.

Cockles tend to be sandy. To get rid of any sand, keep them in a bucket of salty water to help get rid of the sand in their shells. Don't leave them too long or they will suffocate and die. Leave them for about 20 to 30 minutes.

Cockles are found in silty, gravelly and muddy shores. They are fairly close to the surface and can be raked at low water. Islanders have their favourite for gathering cockles – some beaches richer in harvesting them than others. I understand that Chouet in the north of Guernsey is good 'cockle ground'.

Cook as you would mussels in a pan, shaking till they have opened.

Shelled cockles can be stir-fried in the wok. They can be used in sauces for pasta and rice and can be included in a platter of 'fruits de mer'.

Cockles with Potato Salad

Serves 4
1½ kilos / 3 lbs cockles
500g/1 lb new potatoes
3 spring onions

1 tbsp chopped parsley
half a lemon
Olive oil
Salt and pepper

Cook the potatoes till tender. Drain and cool.

Wash the cockles in water, leaving them in a final rinse of salty water for about 30 minutes for them to clean themselves. They tend to be sandy.

Cook them in a large saucepan with a little water. Shake them till all have opened. This takes about 5 minutes.

Drain them into a colander, saving the juice. The juice may have sand in it so strain it through a very fine sieve or piece of muslin. Remove the meat from the shells.

In a small pan, fry the sliced spring onions in a little olive oil. Add the reserved juice. Simmer till reduced to about 4 tbsp. Remove from the heat. Add the chopped parsley, reserving just a little for garnishing. Season, adding the lemon juice.

Slice the potatoes between four plates. Scatter the cockles on top. Pour over the spring onion, parsley and lemon juice.

Cockles in Cream

Serves 4

$1\frac{1}{2}$ kilos / 3 lbs cockles	Juice of 1 lemon
150 ml/ 5 fl oz double cream	1 tbsp chopped parsley
30g/1 oz butter	2 shallots
4 tbsp white wine	Salt and pepper

Wash the cockles several times in fresh water. Leave for about 30 minutes in the final water to clean them of as much sand a possible.

In a large pan, cook the cockles with a little water, shaking the pan till they are all open. About 5 minutes.

Strain, reserving the juice. Pass it through a fine sieve or muslin. Reduce it by two-thirds.

As the juice reduces, remove the meat from the cockles.

In a pan, fry the chopped shallot in the butter. Add the cockles, the juice and white wine. Remove from the heat, season and add the cream.

Share between four plates. Garnish with parsley.

LIMPET

Limpets	*Patella vulgaris*
Guernsey French	*fllie* (f)
Jersey french	*baîni* (f)
French	*bernicle* (f), *lepas* (m), *patelle* (f)

A limpet has a ribbed conical shell up to 5 cms in diameter. Its colour ranges from shades of brown to grey with a smooth creamy undershell. Under the shell is a strong muscular foot, and a mouth with a strong rasping tongue.

They are widely found on rocks in mid to upper tidal levels. When covered by the sea, they move around feeding on seaweeds but at low tide they stay put clinging to their bit of rock. They are extremely difficult to dislodge, hence the name 'limpet mines'!

When collecting limpets, surprise is important because if you don't get it off first time, you might as well give up. An old paint scraper, a blunt knife or even a stone will help remove them. Avoid collecting limpets from rocks near sandy shores as there will probably be grit in them.

I have never seen them on the fishmonger's slab but no doubt they do make an appearance.

It took me ages before I tried them but I felt I had to.

~   ~   ~

Casseroled Limpets

Serves 4

$1\frac{1}{2}$ kilos/3 lbs limpets in their shells (Approximately 15 per person)

30g/1 oz butter

2 rashers bacon	Spike of rosemary
2 tomatoes	30g/1 oz plain flour
1 onion	150ml/5 fl oz red wine (optional)
2 cloves garlic	Salt and pepper

Soak the limpets in a bucket of salty water (2 tbsp) for 2-3 hours. This cleans them.

Next simmer the limpets for 10 minutes in water that has a handful of herbs and crushed garlic.

Cool and remove the shell.

Fry the chopped onion and garlic in butter. Add the limpets, chopped bacon, rosemary, chopped tomatoes and seasoning. Sprinkle with flour and mix it in.

Cover with red wine and a little water. Cook in a moderate oven for about $1\frac{1}{2}$ hours.

Check regularly, making sure there is liquid. The aim is to have a thick rich gravy.

Serve with mashed potato.

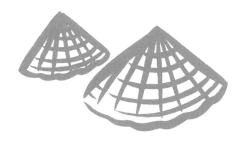

MUSSEL

The Mussel	*Mytilus edulis*
Guernsey French	*moule* (f)
Jersey French	*moûle* (f), *chuchette* (f), *becque-dé-corbin* (f), *orté dé geniche* (m)
French	*moule* (f)

Mussels are a familiar sight at the fish-mongers. The mussels we buy are farmed. The commonest way of rearing them is by suspending ropes from rafts, to which the mussels attach themselves. They will attach themselves to anything that is available – for example jetties, rocks and hulls of ships. They filter their food from the water that flows past them.

The best time for mussels from our waters is September to April but they are available all year round.

If they have to be stored, store them for up to 24 hours under a wet piece of sacking or seaweed. Don't allow them to become dry. Alternatively, don't keep them in still sea water as they will suffocate and die.

Wash and scrape away any fibrous beard before cooking. Discard open or damaged ones.

The most popular recipe for mussels must be Moules Marinières - (mussels cooked in white wine). Cooked this way, I'm sure that many of us are reminded of happy holidays.

Moules Marinière

For 4 people
2 kilo/ 4lbs mussels
1 onion,
30 g/1oz butter

2 cloves garlic
3 tbsp chopped parsley
150ml /5fl oz white wine
Salt and pepper

In a large saucepan, very gently simmer the finely chopped onion and garlic in the wine for 10-15 minutes. I don't add any water as a lot will come out of the mussels and you only have to reduce it later.

Now add the cleaned mussels, put the lid on and allow to steam gently for 5 minutes. Shake the saucepan now and again. Tip into a colander to drain, reserving the liquor. Discard any that have not opened.

If necessary, boil the liquid until reduced so that you have about 150 ml/5 fl oz. Gradually whisk in the butter, add half the parsley and season.

Tip the mussels into a large bowl, pour the sauce over and sprinkle with the remaining parsley. Ladle into warmed bowls.

Crusty bread and a chilled Muscadet are all that is needed.

In Normandy, cider may be used instead of wine. Cream is stirred into the sauce instead of butter.

To eat mussels it is perfectly acceptable to use an empty, hinged shell between your finger and thumb to extract the meat from the mussels. Don't forget a large empty bowl for shells and at the end a bowl of warm water to rinse your fingers.

Mussels in a Saffron Cream Sauce

This is the dish that I enjoyed in the small town of Combourg in Normandy. It was so delicious that I have tried to recreate it.

For 4 people

2 kilos/4lbs mussels	1 medium carrot
Sauce	1 stick celery
A good pinch of saffron threads	1 medium onion
or $\frac{1}{2}$ tsp of powdered saffron	6 cloves
Failing saffron, use $\frac{1}{2}$ tsp of turmeric	1 tbsp freshly chopped coriander
	275ml/10 fl oz milk
60g/2oz butter plus a knob	250g/8 oz basmati or long grain rice
30g/1oz flour	A little chopped parsley for garnishing
2 tbsp double cream	Salt and pepper

Before cooking the mussels put the saffron strands in a cup and cover with boiling water. Leave to infuse for about half an hour – until you get a rich amber liquid.

Place the mussels in a large pan. Cook over a high heat, shaking them now and then until they have opened – about 5 minutes.

Strain, reserving the liquor. When cool enough to handle, remove the shells.

To make the sauce
Place the milk in a saucepan along with the chopped carrot, celery, onion and cloves.

Simmer for 20 minutes.

For the rice, heat a saucepan of salted water to boiling point, add the rice and boil gently for 9 minutes. As it cooks, start the sauce.

Melt the butter then add the flour. If using powdered saffron or turmeric, add now. Gently cook the roux.

Strain the infused milk into a measuring jug and add the strained cooking liquor to make up a good 290 ml/ 10 fl oz. Gradually add to the roux, until you have a creamy sauce. Add the infused saffron water, including the threads and the chopped coriander. Check seasoning.

Strain the rice, return to the saucepan and add a knob of butter. Cover.

Reheat the mussels in a little butter. Reheat the sauce and add the cream.

On a serving dish, coax the rice into a mound. Pour the mussels over, covering them with the rich golden sauce. For the final garnish, scatter a little chopped parsley and serve.

A green salad with some rocket leaves for their pepperiness or the mop-headed, curly-leaved frisée endive, whose slight bitterness balances the richness of the sauce.

Stuffed Mussels with Courgettes

For 4 people
Approx 10 mussels per person, depending on size – of appetites too

120g/4oz white breadcrumbs	1 tbsp chopped coriander
2 tbsp chopped parsley	60g/2oz butter
1tsp chopped lemon thyme	1 egg
1tbsp scissored chives	Tabasco or Worcester sauce
1 lemon	Salt and pepper
2 rashers streaky bacon	Lemon Dressing
1 small onion	Juice from 2 lemons
2 medium tomatoes	4 tbsp olive oil
1kilo/2lbs courgettes	Salt and pepper

First of all, clean the mussels and then cook in a very little water. Shake now and again until they have all opened, about 5 minutes. Discard those that haven't. Let them cool.

In a little butter, gently fry the finely chopped bacon.

Place the breadcrumbs in a bowl. Add the chopped thyme and half the chopped parsley and finely grated lemon rind from 1 lemon and the cooked bacon.

Season, adding one or two drops of Tabasco or Worcestershire sauce.

Bind with one beaten egg.

Take a mussel, one at a time. Remove the mussel meat taking care to keep the shell intact. Take 1 tsp of stuffing placing it in half of the shell. Ease the mussel into the stuffing.

Gently close it and tie with a piece of string. I use a rubber band to keep the mussel shut before tying it.

If you have raffia to tie the mussels, use it in preference to string. Do this to all of them until you have a pile of little parcels. The mussels with the raffia tied round look faintly Japanese or should I say remind me of a sushi bar.

Courgettes
Chop the onion and fry in butter in the same pan you used for the bacon. Put on a plate and now fry the sliced courgettes. When softening, add the onions and chopped tomatoes. Season, adding 2 tbsp of chopped coriander and a little water. Cover and gently simmer until the tomatoes have become mushy.

Lemon Dressing
Mix the lemon juice and olive oil until well amalgamated. Season.

Just before serving, put the mussels (complete with string or raffia) into a roasting tin. Bake for 5 minutes, in a hot oven, to thoroughly heat through.

When serving, place some of the courgette mixture on each plate and scatter with parsley.

Pile the mussels on top but leave them still tied up. Not only do they look attractive, they are also fun to open.

Lots of crusty bread is all that is needed along with the lemon dressing in a small jug. Pour the dressing into the mussels in case they are a little dry.

ORMER

Ormer, Abalone	*Haliotis tuberculata*
Guernsey French	*ormé* (m)
Jersey French	*ormèr* (m)
French	*ormeau* (m), *oreille de mer* (f)

The ormer is undoubtedly the most renowned Channel Island shellfish. Cooking it slowly for a long time turns it into a rich white delicacy that some people would almost die for! Islanders wax lyrical about ormers and now pay extortionate prices for what was once, in fact, part of the staple diet. It must be admitted, not all are so enthusiastic!

The ormer clings to the underside of rocks and in rocky crevices, up to the low tide mark. It is only permitted to take ormers between 1st January and the 30th April and then only on the day of each new or full moon and on the two days following. It is not permitted to collect ormers by diving which includes using masks, flippers, diving suits, breathing apparatus and, furthermore, no ormer less than 8 cms may be taken.

Rules for gathering ormers do change. It would be wise to consult an up- to-date tide-table issued by the States of Jersey or Guernsey before going ormering.

To protect the remaining stock, strict controls on ormer gathering became necessary in the early 1970s due to serious overfishing of the mollusc that had, by then, become almost a national symbol.

Other factors may have also contributed to the ormer's decline such as degradation of habitat and change of sea temperature.

Sadly, it seems that there are even fewer ormers in Jersey than in the other islands.

Even today, the welfare of the ormer can generate heated debate in the States of Guernsey, the Island's parliament.

The efforts of local fisherman Dick Tostevin at Rocquaine have resulted in success in farming the ormer. Large quantities of 'seed' ormers have been distributed and this seeding of the ormer may lead to a rise in the Guernsey ormer population.

Consequently, undaunted by the rigours involved, at the authorised times ormer gatherers, armed only with a trusty hook and almost religious zeal, continue to pursue the delicacy, endlessly turning boulders while waist deep in sea water, in search of the elusive 'feed'.

In other parts of the world where ormers are found they are known as 'abalone'. They are particularly appreciated in China where dried abalone is reputed to have aphrodisiac properties.

As the French name suggests, the ormer resembles an ear, a convex oval shell with a row of small holes along the curved edge. The outside is grey in colour while the inside is lined with translucent 'mother of pearl'. During Victorian times this mother of pearl had various applications including buttons, jewellery and furniture decoration.

Once home with your precious catch, the cleaning process begins.

The first thing to do is to extract the ormer. Wearing a glove or some protection to the hand, hold the ormer, shell side down in your palm. Slip a sharp knife under the pad, cut around the fibrous centre bit that anchors it to its shell. Ease the ormer out.

Now, with a hard bristled brush, scrub the frilly skirt to remove any grit. Once thoroughly scrubbed and rinsed, place it between two cloths and beat it with a mallet or rolling pin to help tenderise it. Don't smash or pulverise it.

What constitutes 'enough for a feed' in ormer-speak, is an unanswered question. So when it comes to quantities a lot depends on how many have been gathered, their size, size of appetites too! The flesh or meat of ormers is rich. Two or three would be adequate for me.

Cooking varies and every cook has his or her own favourite way. Whatever is added – whether it is bacon, onion, herbs or red wine – ormers are cooked slowly in the oven resulting in a rich dish needing nothing but mashed potato to accompany it.

Casseroled Ormers

First of all toss them in flour. Fry in plenty of butter until golden brown. Place in a casserole.

Now fry a chopped onion and, if you like, cut up pieces of streaky bacon. Once both are cooked, add them to the ormers.

In the buttery pan, sprinkle a tablespoon of flour. Add water, or better still if you have some, a little chicken stock, finally a couple of bay leaves. Bring to the boil, season and pour over the ormers making sure they are well covered. Cook gently for three to four hours. Long slow cooking produces a rich gravy.

You may have to add a little water while they are cooking to ensure plenty of gravy.

All that is needed is a bowl of boiled potatoes. Mash them in the gravy. What a feast!

~   ~   ~

Oyster

European or native oyster	*Ostrea edulis*
Portuguese oyster	*Crassostrea angulata*
Pacific oyster	*Crassostrea gigas*
Guernsey French	*huitre* (f)
Jersey French	*hître* (f)
French	*huître* (f)

Up until about the early 1900's, oysters were fished in the Little Russel. Boats from England sailed here for that purpose.

Oyster beds were found in a few places around Guernsey such as at Les Ameureurs.

George Domaille, a friend from the north of Guernsey, has shown us old beds at Chouet which sadly are no longer used. He goes there to cut *vraic* (seaweed) for his garden.

The best time for oysters is during the winter months. During summer, they are spawning. They look fatter because they are full of eggs but are less succulent.

Oysters are sold by the dozen.

If you buy already opened oysters, make sure the juice around them is clear and that they smell of the sea and not a strong fishy odour.

The European or native oyster and the Portuguese oyster are not the oysters we see at the fishmonger's. Although available, the oyster that we see is the Pacific oyster known as the 'gigas'. It is said that the native oyster is the most flavoursome but this may not be absolutely true as oysters acquire the flavour of the water they are grown in.

Inside the oyster's rather rough and ugly exterior is a pearly white interior that is smooth with a curvacious surface that invites the finger to run over the milky-white brittle lining. Too often the shell is discarded without this beautiful interior being given even a single glance.

The oyster, in its natural state, cements itself to rocks, posts, etc. – in fact anything that it can get a hold on. It is found in river estuaries and on rocky coasts. The oyster is extensively farmed.

It seems that traditionally an oyster should be eaten raw. 'Connoisseurs' would, no doubt, consider it sacrilege to cook them.

In France a small fork is given to assist eating them. The custom in England was to eat them straight from the shell. A little messy but it was considered *de rigeur* for a man to have a huge napkin around his neck but hardly beguiling for the fairer sex.

Now we have the choice.

What to drink with an oyster is also debatable. Some say only champagne, others Guinness, others a good dry white wine. A lot depends on where you are and personal preferences but really oysters deserve the best.

This reverence for the oyster was rather tarnished, for me anyway, when one summer we passed through Cancale, in the Bay of Mont St Michel where oysters are reared on a huge scale.

We watched an endless stream of tractors making their way to and from the beach with wire pallets filled with oysters in which they had been reared. These were stacked high and dripped with water as they were taken to the cleaning tanks. There must have been thousands, perhaps millions. In the clean water of the tanks they purge themselves of anything nasty. But it was not a pretty sight and the romantic image – sailing for oysters in Falmouth for example – had gone.

Opening oysters needs skill – or is it a knack? A proper oyster knife is essential plus an old glove or towel to protect the hand. The very rough shell can cause cuts and grazes and the slip of the knife can cause injury.

Do try and open them at home because, if you ask your fishmonger, the precious juice will be lost on the way back or ask him just to ease the shell open so that you can complete the task at home.

Having properly protected your hand, take the oyster with the curved shell in the palm of your hand. Look for a crevice at the hinged end where you can insert the point of the knife. It may be a bit of a struggle but the shell will open. Now with a sharp knife run it under the oyster, cutting the muscle so that it is no longer attached to the shell. Carefully place on a dish in the half shell so that the juice doesn't spill.

If possible some seaweed makes an excellent bed for the oysters

There are also special oyster dishes.

Now all that is needed is some lemon juice, Tabasco or Worcestershire sauce, but only a few drops. And of course – don't forget only the best to wash them down with.

Oysters à la Marinière

~ from Jersey Nick ~

Serves 4
6 to 8 oysters depending on size
3 courgettes
2 cloves garlic
Oregano, basil and parsley

Oil for frying
2 onions
2 cloves garlic
White wine
Salt and pepper

Place the oysters in boiling water for 1 minute. Shuck.
Fry the chopped onion and garlic. Add the chopped courgette, oregano, basil and white wine. When warm add the oysters and parsley. Serve.

Oysters with Champagne sauce

Serves 4
Allow 5/6 per person
120g/4 oz butter
1 finely chopped shallot
1 tbsp chopped parsley

1 tbsp scissored dill
1 tbsp chopped tarragon
275ml/10 fl oz champagne,
    alternatively a good dry white wine
Salt and pepper

Open the oysters as previously described. Remove the oyster and save the juice. Set aside.

Melt the butter in a pan. Add the chopped shallot and cook until transparent. Gradually add the champagne and juice from the oysters, whisking until absorbed by the butter. Continue to boil until reduced by half.

Add the chopped herbs. Season.

On serving, add the oysters and warm through.

Spoon the oysters on each plate surrounded by the buttery sauce.

Little is needed – just a bowl of wedges of lemon and chunks of bread.

Angels on Horseback

Angels on Horseback are a savoury, usually served at the end of the meal. Somehow I feel that this dish would not be greeted at the end of a meal with the delight it once was. Times change!

Served at the beginning of the meal when one's appetite is sharp is, I feel, better. It's a treat and deserves to be lingered over.

Once again, the number of oysters depends on size of the oysters.

Take approximately 4 per person.

Having removed the oysters from their shell, season them with salt and pepper and a few drops of lemon juice and anchovy essence.

Wrap them in streaky bacon making sure the join is underneath.

Grill for fine minutes under a high heat until the bacon is cooked and sizzling.

Serve as they are with a garnish of watercress or on hot buttered toast.

They are excellent impaled on a cocktail stick and served with an aperitif.

Angels on Horseback must be King of the cocktail nibbles brigade.

Grilled Oysters with a Mushroom and Parmesan Topping

Serves 4

4/5 oysters per person
1 small onion
1 clove garlic
60g/2 oz mushrooms
2 tbsp white breadcrumbs
1 tbsp chopped parsley
1 egg

150ml/ 5 fl oz cream
1 generous tsp flour
Tabasco
1 tbsp finely chopped fresh ginger
30g/ 1 oz grated Parmesan cheese
30g/ 1 oz butter
Salt and pepper

Finely chop the onion and garlic. In a small saucepan fry both in melted butter.

Add the finely chopped mushrooms and ginger. Season with salt and pepper and a few drops of Tabasco.

Add the egg yolk and flour. Mix well. Now gradually add the cream, holding back if necessary as you want a thick sauce.

Place the oyster shells on a heat-resistant oyster dish, crinkled foil or rock salt. Place an oyster in each shell. Spoon over the mixture.

Whisk the egg white until stiff and add the breadcrumbs. Place a blob on each oyster, smoothing a little. Sprinkle with the Parmesan cheese.

Alternatively, fill individual ramekin or flattish plates with the oysters. Cover with the mixture, finally the breadcrumbs and Parmesan.

Grill till golden and bubbling.

Crumbed and Fried Oysters

Serves 4
At least 6 oysters per person
2 eggs
30g/1oz fresh white breadcrumbs
1 level tbsp flour

1 tbsp chopped chives
1 tbsp chopped coriander
Salt and pepper
Worcestershire sauce
60g/2oz butter

In a bowl mix the breadcrumbs, the herbs and the flour. Season.

In another bowl beat the eggs.

Dip the oysters into the beaten eggs and then the herbed breadcrumbs. Repeat so that they are well coated.

In a frying pan heat the butter. Fry the crumbed oysters, turning once and shaking the pan to prevent burning and sticking.

Fry in batches. When they are all are done, serve piled on a plate surrounded with wedges of lemon.

A spicy tomato sauce would go well with them.

Scallop

Scallops	*Pectinidae*
Guernsey French	*vannet* (m)
Jersey French	*couinne* (f), *pitonne* (f), *scallope* (f), *vanné* (m)
	Queen scallops – *callifichieaux* (f)
French	*coquille* (f)

The main distinction between scallops and other bivalves, e.g. mussels, is that scallops travel, often great distances when migrating. They have a strong muscle which opens and closes their shells forcing them along in convulsive jerks. Scallops have eyes – mussels don't.

They are found in sandy gravelly areas and fairly shallow offshore waters, from the Atlantic down to the Mediterranean.

There used to be prolific scallop beds between Guernsey and Jersey which remained undisturbed for hundreds of years as there was no demand. Suddenly they became popular and down went the divers and along came the dredgers.

During the 1970's and 80's tons were fished until the beds were exhausted.

Slowly numbers are increasing as protection laws have been introduced.

The two main edible scallops locally are the Great scallop and the Queen scallop. The former has one flat shell and one convex whereas the Queen has two convex shells. The Queen is smaller.

Scallops are best during the winter months.

Try to buy them in the shell or seek assurance from your fishmonger that loose ones have been freshly removed from their shells.

Scallops are one shellfish that can be opened and displayed on their shell.

I like to see scallops served in its shell. The shell is very interesting with its fluted ridges fanning out from the base and the rich rusty reds of the shell are worthy of more than a passing glance.

Open scallops using the point of a knife, inserting it where the two shells join, then slide the blade under the flesh.

Free the meat – the frilly mantle along with the black stomach sac needs to be removed by pulling it free. This comes away quite easily and you are left with the white muscle and coral. Seperate these two as the coral needs only a whisper of heat to cook it.

Coquille St Jaques is a household name but there is also an interesting story behind it.

Medieval Christians would make the long pilgrimage to Santiago de Compostela in Spain to pay homage at the tomb of St Jacques. The pilgrimage originally started from St James' in London with pilgrims joining it as it made its way to Spain.

On arrival, the pilgrims would buy a scallop and, having eaten it, would attach the shell to their hat or garment as a sign that they had made the long hard journey.

Having mentioned St Jacques I will start with that well-known recipe, although there are many variations under the same name.

Coquille St. Jacques

Serve 4

Scallops are very rich so allow just 3 per person

90g /3oz butter	150ml/5fl oz white wine
120 g /4oz mushrooms	1 tbsp chopped chives
90g / 3oz fresh white breadcrumbs	1 level tbsp flour
Finely chopped clove garlic	2 tbsp cream
2 tbsp chopped parsley	Salt and pepper

Scallops tend to be sold out of the shell but, if you can get shells from your fishmonger, it is a very attractive way of serving them.

Prepare the scallop shells (propping them with crinkled foil to stop them capsizing). Alternatively use small ovenproof dishes.

Poach the white meat of the scallops in a frying pan, in the white wine for 4 to 5 minutes. When all but cooked, add the coral, which only needs a few moments of gentle heat to cook. Drain the liquor and keep it for the sauce. Remove the scallops and keep warm.

In the same pan, fry the finely chopped mushrooms and clove of garlic in a knob of butter.

In a small saucean melt the remaining butter and add the flour to make a roux. Gradually add the liquor and stir until smooth and bubbling.

Season. Add the chopped parsley, chives, and mushrooms. Remove from the heat, finally adding the cream.

Quarter the cooked scallops. Place the meat in the scallop shells or dishes along with the coral.

Spoon the sauce over, sprinkle with breadcrumbs and dot with butter. Brown under a hot grill until bubbling.

Serve with bread and a small dish of lemon wedges. This helps to cut the richness of the dish.

There are variations to this recipe. Some recipes suggest no mushrooms while others suggest tomatoes.

Grilled or Barbecued Scallops

It is said that the best way of cooking scallops is to grill or barbecue them.

Beforehand the scallops can be marinated or simply coated with melted butter. We all have our favourite mixture. Some like a touch of Tabasco while others prefer lemon juice, herbs, anchovy, oriental sauces, curry pastes and so on.

To grill: Place in the grill pan. Brush with a little melted butter. Season then grill them under a hot grill for 2 mins on each side.

Another variation is to grill just the white part and serve the coral in a sauce.

If barbecuing, once again care must be taken not to char them. Barbecue them in your favourite way, either on skewers or on a wire rack but, once on the barbecue, don't overcook or they will toughen.

As with other shellfish, bacon goes well with scallops and if cooking on a skewer the scallop can first of all be wrapped in a piece of streaky bacon. Another way is to use a potato peeler to make thin strips of courgette. Wrap the scallop in the strip of courgette, thread on the skewer or kebab stick and grill.

~   ~   ~

Scallops in a Creamy Sauce with a Rice Halo

Serve 4
3 scallops per person
120g /4oz butter
150ml /5 fl oz double cream
150 ml /5fl oz dry white wine
1 tbsp vermouth

1 tbsp flour
3 rashers of smoked streaky bacon
Salt and pepper
Nutmeg
Scissored chives
250g /8oz Basmati rice

Start by boiling the rice in salted water. Strain and add a walnut-sized piece of butter. Place in a well buttered ring mould. Push the rice firmly down. Cover with foil. Keep warm in a bain-marie or cool oven.

Cut the rashers into strips and fry till crisp. Keep warm.

Slice the white of the scallops thinly and keep the coral to one side. Melt half the butter and gently fry the sliced scallops for 2 minutes. When all but cooked, add the coral. Season with a grating of nutmeg. Add the wine and vermouth and heat through.

With a slotted spoon, remove the scallops to a serving dish, cover with foil and keep warm. Sprinkle the flour over the mixture in the pan. Whisk so that there are no lumps. Bring slowly to the boil. Stir until thick and then add the cream. Check the seasoning.

When ready to serve, carefully remove the rice by running a knife around the tin. Place your serving plate on top. Invert and carefully remove the tin.

Tip the scallop mixture into the centre. Sprinkle with chopped parsley or scissored chives and roughly crumbled bacon.

Saffroned Scallops

Serves 4
3 scallops per person
60g/2oz butter
1 shallot
1 clove garlic
150ml/5 fl oz cream
150ml/5 fl oz dry white wine

Juice of half a lemon
A good pinch of saffron threads
half tsp powdered saffron or
30g/1 oz flour
1 tbsp chopped parsley
Salt and pepper

Place the saffron strands in a teacup or similar and cover with boiling water.

Leave to infuse for at least 15 minutes.

Separate the coral from the scallops and put to one side. Fry the white meat for a few minutes in the butter, adding the coral at the last moment. Remove from the pan and keep warm.

In the same pan, fry the chopped shallot and clove of garlic. Add the flour and powdered saffron (if using) and mix well. Add the lemon juice, wine and saffron water (I add the threads as well). Season and heat until bubbling and then add the cream.

Place the scallops on plates. Pour over the bubbling sauce, sprinkle with parsley and serve.

Scallops in a Noilly Prat Sauce

Serves 4

3 or 4 scallops per person depending on the size of the scallops and
appetites   3 shallots
150ml/5 fl oz Noilly Prat   1 lemon
275 ml/10 fl oz fish stock   1 tbsp chopped chives
150ml/5 fl oz double cream   30g/1 oz butter
60g/ 2oz butter   Salt and pepper

Marinate the scallops in the Noilly Prat, lemon juice, salt and pepper for about an hour.

In a wide pan place the fish stock, the marinate (reserving the scallops) and finely chopped shallots. Simmer until the shallot is cooked, about 5 to10 minutes.

Poach the scallops in this liquid for 4 minutes - no longer. Remove with a slotted spoon and keep warm.

Boil the liquid rapidly to reduce it until it is thick and syrupy. Remove from the heat and stir in the cream.

Now beat in the butter piece by piece. The aim is to have a thick and glossy sauce. Add the scissored chives reserving a few as a garnish. Gently reheat.

Place the scallops on individual plates. Pour over the sauce and sprinkle with the remaining chives.

Whelk

Whelk	*Buccinum undatum*
Guernsey French	*coqu'luche* (f)
Jersey French	*coque* (f), *coqueluche* (f)
French	*buccin* (m)

Whelks are plentiful off Jersey, from where they are frozen and exported to the Far East. They are not found in abundance around the other Channel Islands.

The whelk has an elongated conical helical ribbed shell that can range from shades of brown to grey, often striped. It moves like a snail and is a carnivorous scavenger, eating molluscs and worms.

It is the large muscular foot that is eaten. Those with a strong stomach can eat the rest of it!

Whelks need thorough cleaning by scrubbing as the shells tend to be slimy. They also need to be left in a bucket of salty water for a couple of hours to purge themselves.

They can also be bought ready cooked.

I understand that overcooking hardens them.

To cook whelks, make a court bouillon with 1 litre of water. Include some herbs, 2 bay leaves, a chopped onion and carrot. Simmer for 30 minutes. Strain or leave with the vegetables and herbs. Add the cleaned whelks along with plenty of freshly ground black pepper. Simmer for 10 minutes. They are cooked when the pad can be easily removed from the mouth of the shell.

Avoid overcooking.

Having removed the pad, tease them out of their shells with a strong pin, paper-clip or bent piece of wire. Remove any bits you don't like the look of so that you are left with just the meat.

Serve with a dip such as horseradish or tartare sauce.

Alternatively, having removed the meat from their shells, they can be casseroled in a rich tomato sauce. Serve with a bowl of creamy mashed potato.

They can be served baked with garlic butter as for snails.

Or having been cooked, they can be served in their shells as part of a seafood platter.

They can be added to rice dishes such as paella.

Alternatively, they can be minced and with other ingredients made into cakes and fried.

WINKLE

Winkles (Periwinkle)	*Littorina littorea*
Toothed topshell	*Monodaonta lineata*
Guernsey French	*coquelin* (m), *condan* (m), *bigorneau* (m), *colimaçon* (m)
Jersey French	*vlicot* (m), *coque* (f)
French	*bigorneau* (m),

Most of us have grown up believing that a winkle is the small snail with a coiled, conical-shaped shell that we find plentifully around the islands. In fact, what we have are the 'toothed topshells'!

The periwinkle is found in the islands but only in very small numbers.

It is difficult to change customs one has grown up with so I feel that the toothed topshell will continue to be known as a winkle and treated accordingly.

It is a snail with a very strong conical shell. The body has a strong foot and the head has tiny tentacles. They do not cling firmly to rocks like a limpet but just lightly attach themselves. They get rolled around by the sea and survive the roughest storms. They are found all around our rocky coastline. Only the bigger ones are worth eating simply because smaller ones would take forever to coax out of their shells.

Their colour ranges from dark steely grey to brown and brown banded yellow.

Quantities? I wonder if the 'Pint of Winkles' still exists or has metrication put paid to it!

Gather or buy what you think one person could eat and multiply it.

To cook winkles, first make a court bouillon.

Pour 1 litre of water into a saucepan. Add 2 tbsp white wine or vinegar, a sliced carrot, chopped onion and stick of celery, 6/8 crushed black peppercorns, 2 bay leaves, 2 sprigs of parsley or other herbs at hand, 1 tsp salt. Simmer gently so that the vegetables and herbs can infuse for about 30 minutes.

Either strain or use the court bouillon as it is.

Remove the pad that covers the opening of the shell of the winkles. Add them to the court bouillon. Simmer for 5 minutes. Drain and serve.

You will need either winkle picks or a good sized pin or a bent piece of wire to prize them out of their shells.

Not so long ago a group of friends gathered on the cliffs looking out to the Hanois lighthouse. After our picnic, we went down to the rocky shore and gathered from the rock pools a good quantity of winkles. The children thought this was great fun. Of course the winkles come off the rocks easily compared to limpets. Later the winkles were simmered for 20 minutes, strained and were ready to eat. A number of us gathered round and with pins and bits of bent wire coaxed the winkles out. The children loved this especially as having prized it out, it sprang back into its original shape. I was amazed the way the children tucked in, especially Lily, a little two-year old.

Someone brought a rich creamy sauce for the winkles but the opinion was that they were best dipped in vinegar!

Do have a go, it is such fun.

CUTTLEFISH

Cuttlefish	*Sepia officinalis*
Guernsey French	*cannuet* (m)
Jersey French	*seiche* (f), *cônet* (m)
French	*sèche* (f)

Cuttlefish are smaller than squid and not so well known. The shell that once covered them has now become a bone within the body.

It has two long spindly arms and 8 short tentacles lined with suckers, approximate length is 25 cm/10 inches. It lives on the seabed. Cuttlefish can control the colour and texture of their skin.

Cuttlefish spend the winter in deep water in the Hurd Deep area. They migrate to the Granville area in the Bay of St Malo in the spring. They lay their eggs there and in the autumn migrate back to the deeper water to the north. As they migrate backwards and forwards they are caught.

Cuttlefish hunt by night, feeding on small crabs and fishes.

Like the squid it has an ink-sack. It uses the ink as a form of defence. The ink was used for dyeing cloth brown, hence the name sepia.

The sac is easily broken when cuttlefish are caught.

Don't delay in cooking and eating cuttlefish. Eat as soon as possible as uncooked cuttlefish deteriorate quickly.

Cleaning a cuttlefish is interesting and is done in the same way as squid.

My husband and I cleaned one but as it was the first we had done we managed to damage the ink sac from which emerged a rather gooey dark liquid.

Then we weren't sure what were intestines and what were not. We couldn't find the beak, though it did unexpectedly appear. We couldn't get the bone out either but eventually it gave way to our squeezing.

So with a sense of achievment at having cleaned, skinned and washed our cuttlefish, we cut it into strips, the tentacles as well.

Cuttlefish is extremely tender and like squid needs very little cooking.

Squid and cuttlefish dishes are interchangeable.

Cuttlefish with Courgettes

Serves 4
Much depends on size but probably one cuttlefish per person

3 courgettes	Juice of half lemon
2 tbsp tomato pureé	30g/ 1oz butter
Olive oil	1 tsp lemon thyme
Medium onion	1 tbsp chopped parsley
Ground cumin	Salt and pepper

Slice the cuttlefish in strips and fry in butter over a high heat to quickly brown. Season. Put in a dish and keep warm.

In the same pan, fry the chopped onion and garlic in olive oil. Add the sliced courgettes, sprinkle with cumin. Add the lemon juice, lemon thyme, tomato purée and with a little water gently turn until courgettes are cooked.

Just before serving, add the cuttlefish. Reheat for approx. 2 minutes. Scatter with chopped parsley.

~   ~   ~

OCTOPUS

Octopus	*Octopus vulgaris*
Guernsey French	*pievre* (f)
Jersey French	*pieuvre* (f)
French	*pieuvre* (f) or *poulpe* (m)

The octopus is one of the oldest surviving creatures in the world. Ancient tales, stories and experiences of octopus abound. I have a fear of the octopus. This is from having read Victor Hugo's, *Les Travailleurs de la Mer* (*Toilers of the Sea*) at school. Sentences like this are enough to scare any child:

"Suddenly his arm was grasped, and a feeling of indescribable horror crept over him.

Something living – thin, rough, flat, icy and slimy – from the dark depth of the cavity had entwined itself around his arm, and was crawling up towards his breast. Its pressure was like that of a strap being drawn tight, and its steady persistance like that of a drill. In less than a second, a something, he knew not what, but felt that it was of a spiral form, had closed round his wrist and elbow and reached his shoulder, and a pang went through his body below his armpit…"

And so it continues.

My nervousness of the octopus remains. Not only from Victor Hugo's writing but from swimming down at Portelet. My brothers would tell me that congers and octopuses were watching me from the crevices in the jetty wall. Even now, if swimming there, I don't hang around.

During my school days, I did an exchange with a family whose holiday home was in the Chausey Islands. I can vividly remember the boys ganging up on the girls. They used octopuses as their ammunition, whirling them above their heads and then letting them go in our direction!

On another occasion when our second son was born in Tunisia, I was served octopus in the clinic – I knew it was octopus because I could see the suckers!

Enough chat!

From 1899 the common octopus was found in Channel Island waters until 1962/63. During that winter it was very cold, so much so that the octopus was killed along with many other shellfish. It hasn't returned. Only the odd one is found.

The common octopus has a large head out of which protrude eight tentacles. The common octopus has a double row of suckers.

Within its body, it contains a sack of dark brown ink which it can squirt if it needs to disguise its whereabouts. Males are bigger than females.

The body is covered with a sort of warty skin which can change colour and texture to blend in with the background.

The octopus seen at the fishmonger's has been imported from warmer waters.

It is best to go for smaller sizes as they will be tender when cooked.

Having selected your octopus, don't delay cooking it. They do not keep well and should be cooked within 24 hours.

To prepare, start by holding it by the head and with a sharp knife cut the tentacles off below the eyes. Carefully remove the innards and sac from the body, washing it well under running water. Cut the beak away and inspect the tentacles for any bits of grit or other debris.

Depending on the size, it may be necessary to beat the tentacles and body to tenderise them.

Wrap them in a cloth and using a steak mallet or rolling-pin gently beat them. Don't overdo it.

Casseroled Octopus

Serves 4
1kilo / 2lb octopus – if it hasn't been cleaned, allow extra weight
1 kilo/ 2 lbs fresh tomatoes
2 medium onions
2 fat cloves garlic
1 large glass red wine
Handful of herbs such as thyme, sage, rosemary and 2 bay leaves
60g/2oz butter
2 tbsp olive oil
Salt and pepper

Blanch the octopus by plunging in boiling water. Simmer for 5 mins.

When cool, peel the dark skin from the body, scraping it clean. As mentioned above, if you have a large one, beat the body with a mallet or rolling pin. Cut both body and tentacles into finger-sized pieces, about 5cm/2 ins.

Gently fry in butter, oil or butter/oil mixture until golden brown. Lift out and keep warm.

Fry the sliced onions and garlic until transparent and place in a casserole with the octopus on top.

Roughly chop the tomatoes and add to the casserole along with the roughly chopped herbs and bay leaves. Season. Add the red wine. The ink as well, if you wish.

Cover and cook gently for at least 2 hours in a moderate oven 180C/ 350 F/ Gas 4. Stir, now and again.

Serve with plain boiled rice or just lots of crusty bread and a green salad.

SQUID

Common or European Squid   *Loligo vulgaris*
                            Loligo forbesi – common in
Guernsey and for sale from September through the winter. Squid
are an enormous family but this one is common in our waters.
Guernsey French   *conet* (m), *conuet* (m)
Jersey French   *cônet* (m), *crépie* (f)
French   *calmar* (m), *encornet* (m)

When dealing with squid, they tend to be called 'calamari' which is Italian for squid but a name we have got used to.

I have to add a note saying how surprised and delighted I was when, in Australia with my three grandchildren all under ten, I took them out for lunch. What did they want? A unanimous 'fried calamari'. I wonder how many of my grandchildren here would want the same.

Squid are abundant throughout the world. They swim in shoals near the surface so are easy prey. If attacked they can swim backwards, squirting their black ink to confuse a predator.

The ink was used for dyeing and writing.

The squid comprises an elongated sac, containing the inner transparent 'quill', from which the head protrudes along with two long and eight short tentacles. There are two fins towards the end of the body which help it swim and act as a rudder. The body is covered with a transparent, pinky-brown mottled skin which is easily removed. The muscle of a fresh squid should be white, not purple or pink.

The best market size is 20cms / 8 inches to 35 cms /14 inches in length.

Squid is available all year round but is at its best during the autumn/ winter months.

They can be bought fresh or frozen.

Frozen squid will normally have been cleaned.

Cleaning is quite easy. If the ink is to be used in cooking then the sac must remain intact.

To clean the squid, hold the body or mantle in one hand. Take the tentacles in the other and gently pull them away from the body. Out will come the surprisingly compact innards. Once removed, cut the tentacles in one piece below the eyes so that you have a circle with the tentacles attached. You will find the ink sac attached to the innards. It is easily recognised as it looks like a small silvery eel. Remove the beautiful transparent quill from within the squid. Remove any innards left behind and rinse. Finally remove the transparent skin which is a pinky mottled colour. The wings can be removed by either pulling or cutting them. Don't discard them as along with the tentacles they can be used in the cooking.

A tip from Herbert Nichols, my fisherman friend, is to soak the squid in milk for half an hour before cooking to tenderise it.

Stuffed Squid

For 4 people
Depending on the size of the squid choose either one per person or two bigger ones

120g /4oz smoked bacon	Salt and pepper
3 tbsp chopped parsley	Worcestershire sauce
4 shallots or 1 medium onion	Tabasco
1 egg	2 cloves garlic
4 tomatoes	1 tbsp fresh chopped oregano
4/5 tbsp breadcrumbs	(or thyme or tarragon)
3 tbsp olive oil	150ml/ 5 fl oz dry white wine

Finely chop two of the shallots or half the onion and fry in 2 tbsp of oil until transparent.

Add the finely chopped bacon and finely sliced tentacles. Cook, stirring for 5 minutes.

Add two of the finely chopped tomatoes. Season and cook for a further 3 to 4 minutes. Remove from the heat. Add the breadcrumbs, the beaten egg, half the chopped oregano and 1 tbsp chopped parsley. Mix well.

Using a teaspoon, stuff the squid until about two-thirds full. Give a few good shakes to encourage the stuffing to go down. Add the remaining stuffing. Push it down so that the squid feels really firm. Close the top with cocktail sticks.

In the same pan, fry the remaining 2 finely chopped shallots or other half of the onion and two finely chopped cloves of garlic in 1tbsp olive oil. Add the remaining chopped tomatoes and oregano.

Season, adding a dash of tabasco and Worcestershire sauce and 150 ml/ 5 floz dry white wine. Simmer until soft.

If the pan is big enough, add the stuffed squid, otherwise place in an ovenproof casserole or dish and cover with the sauce. Cover with foil or a lid.

Simmer gently until cooked approximately 40 minutes. Check from time to time to ensure there is adequate liquid.

If cooked in the pan, lift the squid out onto a serving dish, remove the cocktail sticks, pour the sauce over and sprinkle the remaining tbsp of chopped parsley.

If cooked in a casserole, remove the cocktail sticks. Sprinkle with parsley and serve.

If serving cold: Place on a serving dish, spoon over the sauce, sprinkle with parsley.

Cold stuffed squid may also be sliced and used as part of an hors d'oeuvre.

If using the ink, snip the ink sac and sqeeze the contents into a cup with about 2 tbsp water, mix and then strain into the tomato mixture.

Fried Squid in Batter - Calmar d'Oré

Serves 4

2 medium squid or 4 small ones	60g/2 oz plain flour
Batter	150ml/5 fl oz milk
1 large egg	Salt and pepper

First prepare the batter so that it can relax.

In a bowl blend all the ingredients so that you get a thick batter. Allow to rest for 30mins.

Clean the squid as described. Alternatively, use a cleaned squid.

Cut off the tentacles and then cut the body into rings about half cm or quarter inch in thickness. Cut the tentacles into bite size pieces.

Dip in the batter.

The squid can either be fried in deep oil, alternatively it can be shallow cooked using half oil and butter.

When the oil and butter or oil is hot, carefully place the battered squid in the pan. Cook both sides until golden brown, approx. 1 minute on each side.

If deep frying, carefully lower the squid into the hot oil making sure you don't have too many pieces in at the same time.

Drain on absorbent kitchen paper. Keep warm as you fry each batch.

Serve with wedges of lemon and a green salad.

Breadcrumbs can be used instead of batter.

Dip the squid in egg then breadcrumbs and fry in the same way as above.

SOME
HERBS
STOCKS
SAUCES
BUTTERS
& DIPS

HERBS

Without herbs our meals would be dull indeed!

I grow as many as I can. I enjoy gathering what I need and always have a large patch of parsley – you may have noticed that practically every recipe is garnished with parsley! Not only is it colourful but it is rich in minerals and vitamins too. This applies to all herbs, not only do they look and taste good – each adding its own particular flavour – but they have medicinal properties as well.

We are lucky in the islands as we can grow them ourselves, be it in the garden, in pots or on the window-sill. At the same time, an excellent and extensive variety of herbs are grown commercially from which we can choose.

Herbs play a major role in cooking, along with spices.

The word 'herb' has its origin in the Latin *herba* meaning a grass or other green plant. In cooking, herbs can be dried but, if possible try to find and use the fresh variety. Spices, on the other hand, are almost always used dried. Some plants which are herbs when fresh are spices when dry – coriander, for example.

Below are some of the most popular herbs, many of which I use all the time.

Basil

A herb that has become well known though I feel certain that 50 years ago most of us hadn't heard of it. It is the Greek for 'King' and there is something royal about its distinctive smell and taste. It is an essential ingredient of pesto, that great, thick, Italian sauce used for pasta and fish. It goes especially well with tomatoes.

Bay leaf

This is the laurel with which victors were crowned, hence, poet laureate, and is an essential part of Bean Jar (both Jersey and Guernsey!) but that is another matter.

Often used in a court bouillon, in marinades and with fish in general, particularly baked fish.

Chervil

A delicate herb that can be used instead of parsley. It doesn't like long cooking. It is best sprinkled over salads. It has a slight aniseed flavour.

Chives

Another very useful herb with an oniony flavour but not as strong as onion. Can be snipped or scissored on any savoury dish or salad.

Coriander

A very popular herb which to look at can be confused with flat leaf parsley. Both leaves and seeds are used and give a very distinctive flavour to all savoury dishes. Note that the flavour of the leaves and seeds are not the same. Even the roots can be used giving an intense flavour.

Dill

Both leaves and seeds are used. The leaves can be scissored over salads in sauces and in many dishes. The seeds are crushed releasing their aniseed flavour and can be used in sauces and soups.

Fennel

Another aniseed flavoured herb. Very useful in salads. Both leaves and bulb – which is really a vegetable – can be used.

Garlic

The 'essential herb!' Extremely useful in the kitchen whether to rub a salad bowl, chop in a sauce or pressed to be used in many dishes.

Lemon Grass

A perennial grass from the warmer parts of the Orient. Thanks to globalisation we are learning to enjoy eastern tastes – lemon grass personifies Thailand. Very useful with fish and any curries you might be experimenting with!

Marjoram and Oregano

Closely related; marjoram has a more delicate flavour than oregano. Very useful in salads, soups and sauces, particularly tomato ones.

Mint

There are many varieties but spearmint is the one most widely used in sweet and savoury dishes as well as sauces, salads and dips.

Parsley

Extremely popular and versatile. Both flat-leaved (often known as French or Italian) and curly can be used in all manner of savoury dishes. It can be fried too and is the easiest herb to use for colour and as a garnish. Where would we be without parsley sauce!

Rosemary

Another hardy and versatile herb. Use with meat and fish in many ways. It has good lasting qualities and can be dried.

Sage

Both the green and purple sage are very useful but take care as they are strong flavours. Good in tomato based sauces, stuffings and soups.

Savoury

There are two varieties, winter and summer savoury. They have a strong peppery flavour. Good in sauces and marinades.

Sorrel

It is acidic and is used in sauces, salads and soups. It needs very careful cooking.

Tarragon

The French rather than Russian is used in cooking. Good in sauces, salads and vinaigrettes and many fish and meat dishes.

Thyme

Another versatile and easily grown herb. Comes from a large family of which lemon thyme is another favourite. Very useful in sauces, marinades and soups. Keeps and dries well.

Spices come from hot climates of the world and are dried, although some like coriander can be both fresh and dried. Each and every spice play their part in recipes. They can be mixed in many ways but some do have a special affinity to certain foods, such as rhubarb and ginger. Spices are readily available and I am sure that many of us have wandered around the markets of the world absorbing the pungent smells of spices and herbs. – no doubt buying some as well! Some of the better known ones are caraway, cardamom, chilli, cinnamon, cloves, cumin, ginger, mustard, nutmeg, saffron, turmeric, pepper and vanilla. Many such as pepper have many varieties within the group such as cayenne, white, pink or black. All are available for us to try. Also, if one isn't available then we can use another, spices are very adaptable.

~   ~   ~

STOCKS

Stock is used to enrich a dish or sauce. It is important not to overcook fish stock otherwise it becomes cloudy, sticky and bitter.

Fish Stock

To make about 1 litre:

750g/1lb 8oz bones from white fish. If possible, include the head.
1 medium carrot
1 onion   Bouquet garni
2 sticks celery   6 crushed black peppercorns

Roughly chop all the vegetables. Add the bones, making sure there are no traces of blood. Add the bouquet garni and peppercorns. Cover with a good litre of water. Bring to the boil and simmer for 30 mins. Now and again skim any skum from the surface. Strain and allow to cool.

Shellfish Stock

To make about 550ml/ 20 fl oz

About 750g/1lb8oz shells from crabs, lobster, prawns etc.
1 litre / 40 fl oz water   2 stick celery
1 medium carrot   Bouquet garni
1 onion   6 crushed peppercorns

Make as above, boiling to reduce by half once it has been strained.

Court Bouillon

Like stock but without bones or shell. It is slightly acidic and is 'vegetarian'. To make 1 litre:

800 ml water/30fl oz   2 sticks celery
150ml/5floz white wine   6 crushed black peppercorns
2 tbsp white wine vinegar   1 bayleaf and bouquet garni of fresh herbs
1 medium carrot   1 piece of cinnamon stick or blade of mace
1 onion   2/3 crushed cardamom seeds

Make as for the stocks.

For the cook in a hurry, there are very good stock cubes available.

Sauces, Butters & Dips

The following is a quick guide:

For a thin sauce: 275 ml/10 fl oz liquid use 15 g/ half oz plain flour

For a thick sauce: 275 ml/10 fl oz use 30g/1oz plain flour

White Sauce

To make 275 ml / 10fl oz

> 30g/1oz butter
> 30g/1oz flour – less if you want a thinner sauce
> 275ml/10floz creamy milk
> salt and pepper

Melt the butter, add the flour and mix to a roux. Away from the heat, gradually add the milk, stirring till smooth. Gently bring to the boil, season and cover. If it seems lumpy, give a good stir with a wire whisk - does wonders.

Béchamel

Before making the sauce, infuse a bay leaf, blade of mace, bouquet garni and a little chopped onion in 275ml / 10floz milk for 20 minutes. Strain and use as above.

Parsley

To white or béchamel sauce add 2 heaped tbsps chopped parsley.

Herb: 'aux fines herbs'

To a white or béchamel sauce add 2 tbsps of a mixture of chopped tarragon, thyme, chervil or sage. Use what you might have at hand bearing in mind not to overdo the stronger flavours. But you really can't go wrong, use your favourite herbs or what is available.

Cream

To white or béchamel add 150 ml/5fl oz double cream or *crème fraîche*.

Mushroom

To white or béchamel add 180g/6oz finely sliced mushrooms that have been cooked in 60g/2oz butter. Finally a little lemon juice and cream and a grinding of black pepper.

Cheese

To white or béchamel add 2/3 heaped tbsp grated Parmesan.

Sorrel

Care must be taken not to overcook the sorrel otherwise it goes grey and turns into a sludge. Add the de-stalked and washed leaves to a little melted butter in a pan. Shake until wilted, drain. Reduce the liquid to syrup. Chop the leaves. Add the chopped leaves and the syrup to the white sauce. Season.

Velouté Sauce

Velouté can be made using fish, veal or chicken-based stock. It needs care and attention and must slowly reduce, so an hour is needed to finish it.

To make 275 ml / 10 fl oz

60g/2oz butter	150ml/ 5 fl oz double cream
60g/2oz flour	90g/ 3 oz mushroom stalks (optional)
550 ml /20fl oz (1 pint) fish stock	

Start by gently boiling the fish stock with the chopped mushroom stalks. The stock needs to reduce by half. Strain the stock.

Melt the butter. Add the flour to make a roux. Add the stock and stir until smooth. Season. Finally add the double cream.

If you prefer a slightly tart flavour then use *crème fraîche*.

Mustard

To a velouté, add 1 tbsp Dijon/ French mustard.

Au Normand

Make as for a velouté but use cider (not sweet) instead of the fish stock and add 2 tbsps crème fraiche.

Au Vin Blanc

Make as for velouté but instead of fish stock, use dry white wine. Alternatively, use half dry white wine and half fish stock. Once the sauce is made, add 2 tbsps cream or crème fraiche.

Cream Sauce

This is quite simple and takes very little time.

Heat 275ml/10fl oz of the freshest double cream, (if you find that too rich use half crème fraiche and half double cream). Whisk in very gently, bit by bit, 180g/6oz butter. Take your time making sure the butter is well emulsified before you add the next knob. Season.

Just before serving, reheat and add a mixture of herbs, especially tarragon and a little lemon juice.

Spicy Tomato Sauce

1kilo / 2 lbs ripe tomatoes	1 small red chilli – fresh or dried
1 onion	3 bay leaves
2 cloves garlic	Olive oil

In a heavy duty saucepan or small casserole, fry the sliced onion and garlic in 2 tbsp olive oil. When transparent, add the deseeded and chopped chilli, bay leaves, two or three sprigs of thyme and the chopped tomatoes. Add a little water, season with salt and pepper and simmer for about an hour. When thoroughly mushy, sieve or mouli. Check for seasoning, you may need a few grains of sugar to take away the acidity.

Hollandaise Sauce

I used to fight shy of Hollandaise because of the fear of it curdling and because it was so difficult to keep warm until needed. Now with blenders and food processors, life is much easier but, of course, it can still be made by hand. This recipe makes approximately 150 ml / 5 fl oz.:

3 tbsp white wine vinegar	3 tbsp water
4 black peppercorns	1 bay leaf
3 egg yolks	180g/6oz unsalted butter
Salt	

Boil the vinegar, water, peppercorns and bay leaf until reduced to 1 tbsp.

If making by hand, place a bowl in a saucepan of barely simmering water. Add egg yolks and the cooled reduced liquid. Thoroughly mix and then bit by bit add the butter. If you prefer, you can melt the butter gradually adding it to the yolks. Season.

If you aren't going to use it straight away put it to one side to keep warm but not hot.

Stir it now and again to keep it smooth and creamy.

To make it in a blender or food processor: Pop in the egg yolks, start whizzing. Add the cooled vinegar liquid.

In a steady stream, add the melted butter till thickened. Place the creamy mixture in a bowl, cover with cling film. Place in pan of warm (not hot) water, away from any heat, stirring occasionally to keep it smooth and creamy.

Don't let the sauce get hot, this will invite curdling.

If your sauce should curdle, whisk in 1 tbsp cold water and if that doesn't work, start again by placing an egg yolk in a clean basin and then gently add the curdled Hollandaise. It doesn't take long.

Béarnaise Sauce

This is similar to Hollandaise but with more of a flavour of herbs.

4tbsp tarragon or white wine vinegar
4tbsp dry white wine   120g/4oz butter
1 shallot   3 egg yolks
Handful of chopped parsley and tarragon

Roughly chop the parsley, tarragon and shallot. In a small saucepan, pour the white wine vinegar and white wine. Add the herbs and shallot. Simmer gently till reduced to 2 tbsp of liquid. Strain into a double saucepan or bowl in a pan of hot water.

Add the yolks and stir or whisk till well emulsified.

Using a wooden spoon, beat in the butter little by little. Season.

Put to one side, stirring occasionally to keep smooth and creamy.

Just before serving add 1tbsp each of chopped tarragon and parsley. This sauce doesn't need to be served hot, tepid is better. This helps to avoid curdling. If it does curdle, remedy it in the same way as for Hollandaise.

Béarnaise can be made in the same way as Hollandaise using a blender or food processor.

Peanut Sauce

180g /6 oz raw peanuts
Piece of peeled and grated fresh ginger – about 1 heaped tsp
6 stems of fresh coriander (2 tbsp chopped coriander)
1 clove garlic
1 small red chilli, seeded and chopped
Juice of 1 lemon

2 tbsp sesame oil
Salt and pepper

Place the peanuts in the food processor with a little lemon juice. Whizz adding more lemon juice as you go. While still thick, add the remaining ingredients and whizz again. If still very thick, add a little hot water but you must aim for a thick but manageable sauce.

Mayonnaise/ Herb Mayonnaise

Mayonnaise is the basis of many sauces.
It is so easy to make and infinitely better than the bought product.

2 egg yolks
1 heaped tsp Dijon mustard
1 tbsp wine vinegar or lemon juice

275 ml/10fl oz olive oil
Salt and black pepper

Place the yolks in a bowl, blender or food processor along with the mustard, vinegar and seasoning. Mix until smooth and then very slowly add the olive oil until thick.

If too thick, gradually add 1 tbsp cold water till you have the consistency you want.

If it should curdle, start with another egg yolk in a clean bowl and slowly add the curdled mayonnaise.

For Herb mayonnaise, just choose the herb(s) you feel like/ have at hand, chop, and carefully fold in.

Tartare Sauce

150ml/5fl oz mayonnaise
2tbsp chopped parsley
1/2 finely sliced spring onions,
depending on size and how
oniony you like it

1tbsp chopped gherkin
1tbsp chopped capers
Seasoning and a dash of lemon
juice

Mix all the ingredients together. If you like a spicy sauce, add a few drops of Tabasco.

Rémoulade Sauce

True rémoulade should be made with hardboiled egg yolks and a raw yolk.

2 hardboiled egg yolks + 1 raw	1 tsp chopped gherkins
1 tsp wine vinegar or lemon juice	1 tsp chopped capers
1 tsp french/dijon mustard	1 tbsp chopped tarragon
150ml/5 fl oz olive oil	

With a wooden spoon, gently crush the hardboiled yolks until no lumps remain. Add the mustard, the raw yolk and finally the vinegar or lemon juice. Mix until smooth and creamy.

Gradually stir in the olive oil, drop by drop, as for mayonnaise. Finally, add the capers, gherkins and tarragon. Season.

Aïoli

6 cloves garlic	1tbsp lemon juice
3 egg yolks	1 tbsp Dijon mustard
150ml/5fl oz olive oil	Salt and pepper

Push the cloves of garlic through a garlic press or flatten them with a wide-bladed knife. Remove any fibres.

Place the garlic in the small bowl of the food processor. Add the egg yolks and mustard and give a quick whizz. Add the olive oil as for mayonnaise, finally the lemon juice. Season.

Adjust the number of cloves of garlic according to taste.

Aïoli can be made by adding crushed garlic to mayonnaise.

Always use garlic as fresh as possible. If it looks old or wrinkled or is beginning to sprout, don't use it as it can cause indigestion. It will also give a slightly acrid flavour.

Rouille

This is a very Mediterranean sauce. The word comes from the french *rouille* – rust – which of course is the colour of the sauce. There are many versions and they all tend to contain a concentration of red peppers, saffron and chilli. Rouille goes particularly well with all sorts of fish and fish soups.
I shall give you two versions, the second being my favourite.
For a bowl enough for 4 people:

First Version –

2 red peppers	150ml/5fl oz olive oil
3 cloves garlic	lemon juice
1 small red chilli	salt and paprika
2 tbsp white breadcrumbs	

Grill or roast the peppers and chilli so that the skin blackens and blisters. The cloves of unpeeled garlic can also be grilled or roasted. When the peppers and chilli collapse and look roasted, they are ready. Squeeze the cloves of garlic and if they feel soft, they are also cooked.

Peel and deseed the pepper and chilli and place in a food processor with the grilled garlic. Whizz until smooth. Slowly add the olive oil and blend until thick. Add the breadcrumbs and lemon juice and whizz until the right consistency. Season with salt and paprika.

Second Version –

A generous pinch of saffron threads or half packet of powdered saffron
1 tbsp lemon juice

2 cloves garlic, peeled and crushed	1 egg yolk
1 heaped tsp Dijon mustard	250ml/8 fl oz olive oil
1 tsp hot chilli sauce	salt and pepper

First pound the saffron threads in a pestle and mortar, then place in a cup with the warmed lemon juice and allow to infuse for about 1 hour.

Place all the ingredients in the food processor, including the saffron.

Give a whizz and then add the oil gradually until it is thick and creamy. Taste for seasoning.

It is a good idea to make it well in advance so that the flavours can develop.

Vinaigrette

This must be the most useful of all dressings. I tend to make it in a small jar. It is easy to and shake and is there when I need it.

As a rule of thumb, I use 1tbsp wine vinegar to 2 tbsp olive oil and 1 tbsp French mustard, salt and pepper.

If I am using vinaigrette for tomatoes, I add a sprinkling of sugar. This cuts the acidity of the tomatoes.

BUTTERS

When it comes to flavoured butters – the reaction tends to be, "I can't be bothered"! I can assure you it is worth the effort. Also, it is the easiest thing to make.

Many of us must have memories of that grilled Dover sole and the little pat of parsley butter!

Parsley Butter –

60g/2oz butter	1tsp lemon juice
1tbsp chopped parsley	Salt

Leave the butter in a bowl in a warm place so that it becomes soft and creamy. Add the chopped parsley, and lemon juice, mix well and chill. What could be easier! There are variations such as mixed herbs, garlic, a few drops of tabasco and so on.

Anchovy Butter –

60g/2oz butter	2 pressed cloves garlic
3 or 4 anchovy fillets	Ground black pepper
1tsp lemon juice	

Allow butter to soften.

Pound the anchovy fillets in a pestle and mortar. Add to the butter along with the pressed garlic, lemon juice and a grinding of black pepper. No salt is needed. Chill.

Anchovy butter goes particularly well with a bland white fish such as haddock or hake.

The next two dips were my introduction to life in the Middle East. We enjoyed them as far west as Casablanca to as far east as Oman.

DIPS

Hommus

Hommus is simple to make. Just remember to think ahead as using dried chick peas is the best way but they have to be soaked for about 10 hours or overnight. Alternatively, tinned chick peas can be used.

The ingredients store well so they can always be at the ready if you wish to make some. All you need are chick peas, tahini paste, garlic, olive oil and lemon juice.

Overnight soak 100g/3 oz dry chick peas.

Next day (or approx. 10 hours later) cover the chick peas with fresh water. Bring to the boil and simmer for 30 to 45 minutes.

Drain, reserving the water and 7 to 8 chick peas for 'decoration'.

Place the remaining chick peas in a blender or food processor. Add 2 tbsp tahini paste, juice of 1 lemon, 2 or 3 cloves garlic passed through a garlic press, 1 level tsp of salt.

Whizz, checking to make sure that the hommus isn't too thick. Add more lemon juice and, if necessary, some of the cooking water until it is fairly smooth and creamy.

Taste to make sure there is enough salt and lemon juice.

When serving, place in a small dish. Smooth the surface with the back of a spoon. Drizzle with olive oil and a shaking of paprika. Pile the reserved chick peas in the centre.

Serve with pitta bread, crisps or raw vegetables that have been cut in chunky match-sticks.

Hommus can be served instead of mayonnaise with baked fish.

Babaganoosh (or M'Tabel)

Another very easy dip to make.

2 aubergine	2/3 cloves garlic
1 lemon	Tahini paste

First of all, using a fork, prick the aubergines all over. This is important otherwise they might explode and you could be left with a mess to clear up and no aubergines!

Roast them in a hot oven for 30 to 40 minutes so that they looked wrinkled and are soft when you squeeze them.

Cut them in half and scoop the flesh into a blender or food processor – my husband likes to make it in a bowl with a fork as he likes a rougher texture.

Add 2 tbsp tahini, the lemon juice and pressed garlic cloves, salt and pepper.

Whizz till creamy but not smooth. Taste as it may need more lemon juice and salt.

Place in an appropriate serving dish, smooth the surface, drizzle with olive oil and decorate with a sprig of mint. Serve with pitta bread, crisps and vegetables cut into chunky match-stick pieces.

Horseradish and Crème Fraîche

2 tbsp horseradish sauce
150ml/5 fl oz crème fraîche
2/3 gherkins

2 tbsp chopped parsley
Dash of tabasco
Salt and pepper

Chop the gherkins, then add the remaining ingredients.
Chill and serve.

Spiced Red Pepper Dip

1tsp ground coriander
2 large red peppers
2 medium tomatoes
1 tsp ground cumin

Juice of half a lemon
2 spring onions
2 pressed cloves of garlic

Roast, grill or barbecue the red peppers until blistered and collapsed. It is worth the trouble as this gives a smoky taste. Cover the tomatoes with boiling water, then skin and chop.

In a blender or food processor place all the ingredients except the spring onions. Whizz till smooth. Place in a serving dish and stir in the finely sliced spring onions.

Guacamole

Guacamole is very simple to make. Additions such as tabasco or chilli sauce can be added to spice it up.

2 avocados
1 pressed clove garlic
Juice of 1 lemon

2 tbsp olive oil
Seasoning

Either very finely chop or mash the avocados. Add the lemon juice, garlic and olive oil. Beat till well incorporated, season, spicing it up a bit if you wish.

~   ~   ~

FRUIT SAUCES

Gooseberry, rhubarb, apple and elderberry are made by reducing the fruit and sieving it with the addition of other flavourings.

Gooseberry

500g/ 1 lb gooseberries
1 lemon
Knob of butter

1 tsp grated fresh ginger (optional)
Sugar – according to taste

Cover the gooseberries with water. Add the sugar and lemon juice. Simmer until collapsed.

Either sieve or whizz in a blender. Add the knob of butter while still warm. This gives the sauce a glossiness.

Rhubarb

500g/ 1 lb
Knob of butter

Sugar
1 tsp grated fresh ginger

Make in exactly the same way as gooseberry sauce.

Apple

500g/ 1 lb Bramley or other cooking apple
Knob of butter   Sugar

Again made in the same way. A pleasing addition is 2 tsp of freshly grated horseradish or ready-made creamed horseradish sauce. Or perhaps a little ground cinnamon or cloves.

Elderberry

250g/8 oz picked elderberries
Sugar

1 Bramley or other cooking apple

Again made in the same way but perhaps with the addition of 1 tsp ground cloves.

~   ~   ~

SALSAS

Salsas are served as an accompaniment to many dishes. They are refreshing and often a bright colour which adds to the attraction of the dish.
I would describe them as a rather chunky dip.

Tomato Salsa

5/6 red tomatoes (the riper the better)	1 tbsp chopped parsley
1 small onion or 2/3 spring onions	1 tbsp chopped coriander
half lemon	Salt and pepper
1 red chilli	

Skin the tomatoes by placing them in a bowl, pouring boiling water over. After a couple of minutes they are ready for skinning. Next cut them into quarters, de-seed and chop fairly finely.

Chop the chilli finely, removing the seeds first. Finally chop the onion or the spring onion.

Add the chopped chilli and onion to the tomato along with the coriander, parsley and lemon juice. Season. Mix carefully. Place in a dish with a final drizzle of olive oil.

Pepper Salsa

You can use either red or green peppers or a mixture.

4 red or 4 green or 2 of each	1 tbsp chopped coriander
2 cloves garlic	1 tsp ground cumin
3 spring onion	1 lemon
1 red chilli	Salt and pepper
1 tbsp chopped parsley	2 tbsp olive oil

Grill the peppers and chilli until blistered and collapsed. You can skin them or leave some of the charred skin on. Cut in half and remove the seeds and finely slice.

In a bowl, put the finely sliced pepper, spring onion, pressed garlic, chopped parsley and coriander. Stir in the lemon juice and 2 tbsp olive oil. Season with ground cumin, salt, and pepper.

Basil Pesto

Pesto is an uncooked sauce which is made by either pounding ingredients in a pestle and mortar or in a food procesor. There are variations but recipes always include basil, pine kernels and parmesan cheese.

60g/2oz basil leaves	150ml/5fl oz olive oil
60g/2oz grated parmesan	2/3 cloves garlic
30g/1oz pine kernels	Salt and pepper

In a blender, whizz the basil, garlic and pine kernels until paste like. Add the parmesan. Gradually add the olive oil as you would with mayonnaise. When thickish, season.

~ ~ ~

Conclusion

I have had great fun putting all of this together.

I hope I have managed to encourage young and not so young to try some of my recipes.

We are aware of our health and what we should and shouldn't eat. Fish must be one of the highest on the list of Good Foods, so why neglect it especially as we are lucky in having it on our doorstep, fresh too.

My next venture is the foods that grow on our islands, cultivated as well as wild. Not just fruit and vegetables but four-legged food as well.

Recently we collected wild spinach, it was delicious and we could feel it was doing us good!

But how many of us know about it. All being well, I will tell you.

~ ~ ~

Acknowledgements

Having been encouraged by my family to put a local fish cook book together, I got to the point when I had to decide whether to keep what I had done to myself or take the plunge and publish. There was a unanimous "go for it Mum"!

Next step? I needed to show it to someone to get their opinion. Our friend and fish expert, Richard Lord, who lives in Guernsey, was encouraging, pointing out that there is always an interest in regional cook books. I found Roger Jones' name in the *Writers' and Artists' Yearbook*. He came to Guernsey and liked what I had written – so the die was cast!

As I put the recipes together, I met many interesting people, all of whom are dedicated to the care and protection of fish and shellfish and the waters around the islands. First of all, there was Herbert Nichols, a retired fisherman. I loved listening to his memories from times past, his life as a fisherman and his knowlegde of patois. Richard Lord taught me much and helped tremendously with the proof-reading.

As a Guernsey girl, my original manuscript was titled *Guernsey Fish Cook Book*. Roger suggested its scope should embrace all the Channel Islands. This meant visiting them. In Guernsey, John Torode and Roger Sendall at Sea Fisheries were very helpful. In Jersey, I met

Simon Boffey, Director of Sea Fisheries and Nick Jouault, a former fisherman and now marine conservationist. In Alderney, I met John Tayleur of the Harbour Office. All helped a great deal.

Jean de Garis gave lots of encouragement, her knowledge of patois was helpful and her artistic talents were put to good use.

I used Marie De Garis' *Dictionary of Guernsey French* and a list of fish from L'Assembllaïe de Guernesiaise. Nick Jouault sent me *Le Vocabulaithe des Païssons en Jerriais* issued by La Société Jersiaise.

I received permission from the French Honorary Consul and Curator of Victor Hugo's house in Guernsey, Madame Veronique Bascule, to use quotations from Victor Hugo.

June Bright, a friend and talented cook, chose recipes at random, tested them and made valuable comments.

Guernsey Herbs grow excellent quality herbs, many of which were used in my recipes.

Finally my long suffering husband. He has read, re-read, corrected grammar and spellings and eaten huge quantities of fish. Recipes have been tested on him. His comments and suggestions have been invaluable. Also his encouragement to persevere.

My sincere thanks to one and all.

Marguerite Paul
September 2001

More books from Seaflower ~

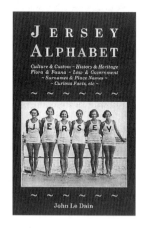

JERSEY ALPHABET

Culture & Custom ~ History & Heritage
Flora & Fauna ~ Law & Government
~ Surnames & Place Names ~
~ Curious Facts, etc ~

John Le Dain

JERSEY in LONDON

Brian Ahier Read

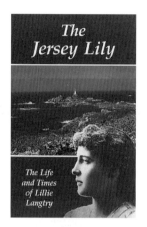

The Jersey Lily

The Life and Times of Lillie Langtry

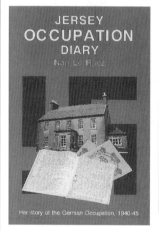

JERSEY
OCCUPATION
DIARY
Nan Le Ruez

Her story of the German Occupation, 1940-45

JERSEY
Not quite British

The Rural History
of a Singular People

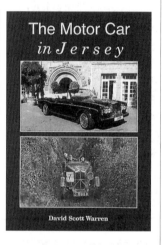

The Motor Car
in *Jersey*

David Scott Warren

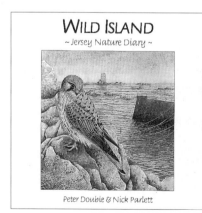

WILD ISLAND
~ Jersey Nature Diary ~

Peter Double & Nick Parlett

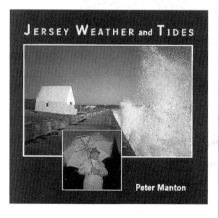

JERSEY WEATHER and TIDES

Peter Manton

Seaflower Books are obtainable through your local bookshop or direct from the publisher,
post-free, on receipt of net price at
1 The Shambles, Bradford on Avon, Wiltshire, BA15 1JS   Tel/fax 10225 863595
e-mail: roger.jones@ex-librisbooks.co.uk   www.ex-librisbooks.co.uk

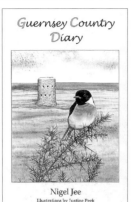

Guernsey Country Diary

Nigel Jee
Illustrations by Justine Peek

NO CAUSE FOR PANIC

Channel Islands Refugees
1940 - 45

Brian Ahier Read

LIFE *on* SARK

Through the year with
Jennifer Cochrane

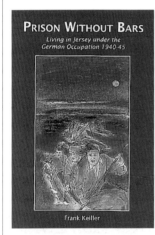

PRISON WITHOUT BARS

Living in Jersey under the
German Occupation 1940-45

Frank Keiller

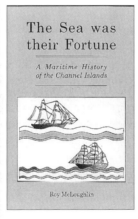

The Sea was
their Fortune

*A Maritime History
of the Channel Islands*

Roy McLoughlin

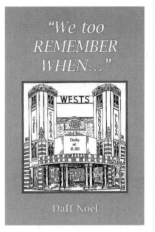

"We too
REMEMBER
WHEN..."

Daff Noël

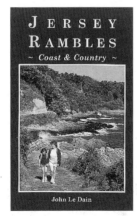

JERSEY
RAMBLES
~ Coast & Country ~

John Le Dain

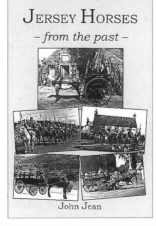

JERSEY HORSES
– *from the past* –

John Jean

John Skinner's
Visit to the
Channel
Islands
August 1827

John Le Dain